WHY
EMPLOYEES
DON'T DO
WHAT THEY'RE
SUPPOSED TO DO
AND WHAT TO
DO ABOUT IT

Other McGraw-Hill Books by Ferdinand F. Fournies

Coaching for Improved Work Performance

Why Customers Don't Do What You Want Them to Do—And What to Do About It

WHY EMPLOYEES DON'T DO WHAT THEY'RE SUPPOSED TO DO AND WHAT TO DO ABOUT IT

FERDINAND F. FOURNIES

Revised and Updated Edition

McGraw-Hill

New York San Francisco Washington, D.C. Auckland Bogotá
Caracas Lisbon London Madrid Mexico City Milan
Montreal New Delhi San Juan Singapore
Sydney Tokyo Toronto

Library of Congress Cataloging-in-Publication Data

Fournies, Ferdinand F.
   Why employees don't do what they're supposed to do and what to do
about it / Ferdinand F. Fournies.
      p.   cm.
   Includes bibliographical references and index.
   ISBN 0-07-134255-9
   1. Supervision of employees.   I. Title.
HF5549.12.F68   1999
658.3'02—dc21   99-11273
                                                  CIP

McGraw-Hill

A Division of The **McGraw·Hill** Companies

  2 3 4 5 6 7 8 9 0 AGM/AGM 9 0 4 3 2 1 0 9

ISBN 0-07-134255-9

Printed and bound by Quebecor/Martinsburg.

McGraw-Hill books are available at special quantity discounts to use as premi-
ums and sales promotions, or for use in corporate training programs. For more
information, please write to the Director of Special Sales, McGraw-Hill, 11 West
19th Street, New York, NY 10011. Or contact your local bookstore.

 This book is printed on recycled, acid-free paper
containing a minimum of 50% recycled, de-inked fiber.

To Betty
My Friend, My Partner, My Wife

Contents

Introduction

The need for effective face-to-face management is becoming more crucial with each decade. Technological advances, as wonderful as they are, have increased the potential and magnitude of the errors an employee can make by merely hitting the wrong key. A $16 dividend check can become a $16,000 check, a phone call to New Jersey can become a call to Russia, and any inventory can be wrong by a factor of ten. Simultaneously, the manager's window of opportunity to prevent or correct errors has decreased at an inverse ratio. Because information is now moving so fast in business, it is becoming blatantly clear that the manager who waits for an employee to announce a problem has waited too long.

Also, the jeopardy confronting managers who discipline employees has become draconian. It used to be that a manager could be demoted if he or she could not deal effectively with employee performance problems. Now a manager could be assaulted or killed by the employee for the same reason. Workplace homicides have increased tenfold nationally in the past decade. In some companies, employees have banded together in a dirty tricks team for the single purpose of making the boss miserable — if not getting him or her fired — and there actually are consultants who help employees do that. A recent study suggests that managers run double the risk of having a heart attack during the week after they fire an employee. And it doesn't look as if the job is going to get easier in the future because of a general social decline in respect for authority and just about everyone else. Colleges are reporting a general decline in student decorum, with students coming to class late and leaving early, reading newspapers, talking on cell phones, watching portable televisions, sleeping, and directing verbal abuse at teachers. Say hello to your future employees.

Managing employees effectively is no longer a luxury if you can spare the time; it may be worth your life.

Fortunately, most people at work do most of what they are supposed to do most of the time. They are cooperative, hard-working, and dependable. Some employees do even more than they are supposed to do: they arrive early and stay late; they are nice to have around. But there are those few bad performers who don't seem to do anything right. Unfortunately, there are also those occasions when even the good performers do it wrong or not at all.

You hear about a statue honoring a statesman unveiled in public to reveal his name misspelled; unapproved currency trading which loses $500 million for a company; a $50 million chemical spill because someone opened a valve instead of closing it; explosive materials loaded on passenger flights that shouldn't be there; an employee fired for the wrong reason, resulting in a $10 million lawsuit. And how about the warning message from the U.S. Army Chief of Staff sent to the Pearl Harbor commander on December 6 warning of imminent attack by the Japanese that was sent regular Western Union instead of by high-priority military communication so the telegram was sitting in Hawaii Western Union as the bombs fell. These things happened because an individual did something wrong or failed to do something right.

Have you ever asked yourself, "Why don't they do what they are supposed to do?" Don't feel bad if you didn't get a good answer; most managers have the same problem.

A similar but larger question, "Why does man do what he does?" has been the burning question for philosophers, poets, and scientists down through the ages. Psychologists offer many theories as possible answers to that question, but in some instances their answers are not answers at all. For example, you have probably heard that man does what he does because he is motivated to do it; the motivation is the reason. Unfortunately, psychologists don't agree with each other on what motivation is or how it operates. Some psychologists believe that motivation must always come from within the person, while other psychologists believe that motivation must come from outside the person. Both appear to present equally convincing theories for their side, but both are confusing.

The nuances of this motivation debate are useless to the manager who is trying to get people to produce a quality product or perform a quality service within the constraints of time, cost, and safety. The literature is confusing to managers searching for a practical answer to the question, "How do I motivate my people?"

In my consulting company, which services clients in industries around the world, we are continuously searching for the answer to that same question because companies pay for the answer. A client company wants to be told how to increase sales or how to improve product or service quality. If the answers we give as solutions are ineffective, we don't get paid.

Unfortunately, our organization's review of the psychological literature has led us, like many others, to conclude that motivation is a difficult thing to describe, much less measure. You can't measure it like blood pressure. It seems that motivation is a term invented to describe "what we don't know" is causing people to do what they do. Because psychologists have difficulty describing specifically why people do what they do, individual managers have much less of a chance in coming up with a workable answer.

Somewhat frustrated, we asked ourselves, "If we can't make up a specific list of why employees do what they do, could we discover why employees don't do what they are supposed to do?" So, about twenty-five years ago we started asking managers in our management seminars, "Why don't your subordinates do what they are supposed to do?" Their answers at first were not very helpful because they were not specific. One common answer was, "Because they are not motivated." When we wrote that down and asked, "Why aren't they motivated?" the response was, "They don't want to do it." When we wrote that down and asked, "Why don't they want to do it?" they would answer, "They are not motivated." So, around in circles we went.

As time went on, we asked better questions. For example, we asked, "Why don't people want to do it, and the answer can't be that they are not motivated?" Managers responded with a lot of different answers, such as, "They don't know why they should do it," or "They think it will not work," or "They don't care." The list of answers got longer.

After doing that for about five years, we noticed something very interesting: the answers didn't change. Although occasionally the answers came out in a different sequence, the completed lists were similar, giving sixteen reasons. We also noticed that whether we were talking to corporate presidents or first-line supervisors, the same reasons were given. For example, the answer, "They think their way is better," was given as a reason for nonperformance by managers of janitors, computer programmers, and vice presidents. We kept coming up with the same sixteen reasons for inappropriate performance. After working with this list over the years, we noticed something even more interesting: almost all of these reasons for nonperformance were controlled by the manager. We also realized that there were two general management causes for most of these reasons for nonperformance:

a. The manager did something wrong to or for the employees, or

b. The manager failed to do something right to or for the employees.

In other words, employee nonperformance occurred because of poor management. What followed was the startling realization that if managers took appropriate action to make these sixteen reasons for nonperformance go away or prevent them from occurring in the first place, the result would be perfect performance.

The first edition of this book was based on a fifteen-year study of reasons for poor performance gathered from over 20,000 managers. In the ten intervening years we have collected information from an additional 5000 managers which supports our original finding that there are specific effective management interventions any manager can use to prevent almost all of those reasons why people don't do what they are supposed to do at work. This is in contrast to the never-ending search for the secret button to push to get people motivated. We found that many managers were already using these interventions effectively without knowing they were doing something special. But when we brought it to their attention, they got better at it. The overwhelming conclusion is that management is an intervention more like bridge building than rain dancing: there is a direct cause-effect relationship between a manager's actions and an employee's performance.

This amazing revelation that there are only sixteen reasons affecting people's performance gives managers a more practical interpretation of this old generalized concept of motivation. The question, "How do I motivate my people?" leads to generalized and nonspecific answers. In contrast, the question, "How do I improve my people's performance?" leads to a targeted analysis of the sixteen causes of performance problems and specific actions you can take to improve performance.

The objective of this book is to tell you how to get all of your people doing what they are supposed to be doing all of the time. You will learn and understand all of these sixteen reasons we discovered why employees don't do what they are supposed to do. You will also learn the specific interventions you can take to deal with each of those reasons to get the performance you want. We will not deal with all of the problems you have in managing people. We will deal only with the sixteen reasons that influence their performance.

If all you are doing now is hiring the best people and putting them on the job with minimum management effort and you are satisfied with their performance, don't bother reading this book. If, however, you think performance should be improved and you are willing to try to improve it, please continue reading.

This book introduces a powerful new management system called Preventive Management. This system uses proactive interventions to prevent problems from occurring vs. the typical problem management approach which merely reacts to solve problems after they occur. My objective is to help you to manage your employees' performance so that fewer performance problems occur, especially when the result of poor performance is costly. Each chapter focuses on a single reason for nonperformance. Each reason, in its various disguises, will be presented first, followed by the preventive solutions (the actions you can take to prevent that nonperformance from occurring).

I wish you good management.

WHY EMPLOYEES DON'T DO WHAT THEY'RE SUPPOSED TO DO AND WHAT TO DO ABOUT IT

Part I

The Hidden Influences That Affect Everyone's Performance

1

They Don't Know
Why They Should Do It

OF ALL THE REASONS FOR EMPLOYEE NONPERFORMANCE, "They don't know why they should do it" is the easiest for managers to accept because it is so logical without explanation. Almost any book, article, or lecture instructing managers how to motivate employees stresses the importance of them "Knowing why." In these modern days of management, you hardly ever hear managers say, "Don't worry about why, just do it," or "We don't have the time to sit around answering all of your questions; just go do what you get paid to do," or "Can you ever do anything without questioning my judgment?" Only dumb managers would say that. Enlightened managers know that it is all right for employees to ask "Why?" Unfortunately, not enough managers make the effort to answer that question *before* it is asked. As a result, employees fail because they don't know why they should do it.

THE PROBLEM

Managers usually describe this reason for nonperformance in different ways:

- They don't think it is important
- They think it is not worth the effort
- They don't want to do it
- They don't have a reason for doing it
- They say, "Why, should I do that?"
- They don't care

In our search for specific information about performance problems a discussion with a manager typically goes like this:

> ME: "Why don't employees do what they are supposed to do?"
> MANAGER: "They don't care."
> ME: "Don't care about what?"
> MANAGER: "Don't care about doing it."
> ME: "Why don't they care about doing it?"
> MANAGER: "They don't know how important it is."
> ME: "What do you mean?"
> MANAGER: "They don't realize how others are affected by what they do."
> ME: "You mean they don't know why they should do it?"
> MANAGER: "Right."

This discussion illustrates a pervasive problem in performance management: managers are not specific enough in analyzing employee performance. The expression "They don't care" could mean employees are "not taking care," which means they are not working carefully, not following the correct procedure, or even abusing their equipment or customers—that is, they are not doing it correctly. Or the expression could just mean employees don't "have a care," which means their thoughts about doing it are not related to the importance of doing it—that is, doing it right or wrong appears to be of no importance to them. The latter person is who we are talking about in this problem situation. Employees with this problem might have been told they should do something, and they might have been told it is important, but they don't know why it is important.

This information about why a specific task or project is important falls into two categories. Category one includes the benefits to the organization for doing a task right as well as the harm to the organization for doing it wrong. Category two includes the benefits to the employees for doing a task right as well as the harm to the employees for doing it wrong. The first category deals with why the task should be done; the second category deals with why that employee should do it. If your employees do not know the consequences in both of these categories, you might face nonperformance because they don't know why they should do it.

These two categories are not of equal importance to everyone, however. For example, a performer's concern about his error, which will cost the organization $100, is quite different from his concern about the same error when he discovers the $100 will come out of his paycheck.

Frequently in business people are required to do things a certain way for reasons that are very clear to managers but are not so clear to employees. Here are some examples for the first category:

○ My boss is really weird. She gets aggravated when you don't grab the phone as soon as it rings.
   —(The reason the telephone should be answered within two rings is because we want to create the image of effective service to our customers.)

○ I would rather make notes after the experiment is finished. Why does everything have to be done her way?
   —(The reason you should make detailed laboratory notes as your experiment progresses is to produce more accurate notes to provide a basis for tracking down errors, as well as to meet the legal requirements.)

○ I don't use sales aids because they cramp my style; besides, I don't need them.
   —(One reason you should use sales aids in your sales presentations is to involve more of the customers' senses, such as sight and touch, in addition to sound.)

○ I think it is a waste of time saving all that scrap.
   —(The reason the scrap should be saved is because it can be melted down and used again.)

○ He makes a big deal about smoking in the laboratory because he is probably a reformed smoker.

- —(The reason for not smoking when oxygen is being used is to prevent an explosion because oxygen is highly flammable.)
- ○ I think it is a waste of time saving on my computer every hour.
  - —(The reason is that your computer could crash, causing the last hour's input to be lost.)
- ○ It seems to me that submitting my expense reports late would save the company money.
  - —(The reason for submitting your expense report on time is so the accountants can track cash flow more accurately.)

The reasons might seem obvious as you read this, but in these real situations, they were not obvious to the employees.

Under the second category, "why that employee should do it," the reasons are quite different:

- ○ To get a good performance rating
- ○ To get paid
- ○ To get a raise
- ○ To get an award
- ○ To learn something
- ○ To get a promotion
- ○ To get a choice assignment
- ○ To get recognition
- ○ To avoid embarrassment
- ○ To prevent the pay from stopping
- ○ To avoid a reprimand

○ To avoid a demotion

○ To avoid termination

You can see that employees who do not understand these reasons for doing a task could, from their point of view, have logical reasons to not do it.

PREVENTIVE SOLUTION

People will do things because you tell them they should do them only as long as you watch them. But you can't (and you shouldn't have to) watch employees all the time. The reason for doing things must be important enough to employees to influence their choices of how to perform when the boss is not watching.

Some automobile drivers will not wear seat belts to save their own lives. These drivers start wearing seat belts, however, after their family convinces them that they are recklessly taking chances that could deny the family their presence sooner than necessary. There are drug addicts and alcoholics who do not take steps to overcome their addiction for their own personal health but subsequently will do so for the benefit of their loved ones. Even individuals attempting suicide because they are dissatisfied with life can be convinced not to commit suicide to avoid the bad effect it would have on their loved ones.

1. Before you put people to work, let them know why they should do the things you pay them to do. The first category includes the benefit to the organization for doing the task right and/or the

harm to the organization for doing it wrong. Describe the relationships between the individual tasks employees perform and how these tasks relate to tasks in other departments to customers, and to the mission of your organization. *Don't rush it.*

2. When you want people to change for the purpose of solving problems or improving quality or productivity:

   a. Explain the problems in detail
   b. Explain the goals in detail
   c. Discuss the solutions in detail
   d. Explain the expected benefit of success and the
   e. Expected agony of defeat

3. When a task is undesirable or difficult to do, or if the immediate consequences of the task are not rewarding, make an extra effort to explain the five items just given. You must be convincing when explaining the long-range benefits for that task being done. For example, in one company, outside salespeople were required to make notes in their customer records after each sales call, but many of them did not do it. Management's stated reason for annotating customer records was to have a complete record of customer activities in case a salesperson left and had to be replaced. As you might guess, that reason was of little interest to any current salesperson. The most important reason for making notes after a sales call is to be able to use the notes to make the next sales call more effective. The notes are not important when the salesperson writes them; they are important in the future when the

salesperson reads them. Switching the emphasis increased record keeping.

4. Don't make the mistake of touting "The Honor and Glory of the Company" as the reason people should do things if all you give them for their work is pay. Unless you are in imminent danger of going out of business and there will soon be no jobs, "Honor and Glory of the Company" translates into "For the Good of the Owners." If workers really received honor and glory for their work, some of them would work for nothing. If you want to give employees something to work for, give them some of the profits.

5. Explain the second category of reasons: why *they* should do a task—that is, the consequences to them for their own performance. Detail for them the personal rewards they gain for performing that task successfully: the increased knowledge, prestige, opportunity, financial reward, comfort, security, and so on. Also detail the personal punishments they receive for not performing that task successfully: the loss of prestige, opportunity, finances, comfort, security, and so forth. Explaining the latter is not only a good action to eliminate reasons for nonperformance, it also fulfills a legal need if you eventually must terminate someone's employment. Judges and arbitrators usually ask, "Did you tell them what would happen to them if they did not perform appropriately?" If the answer is "no," the judge makes you put them back on the job or awards them a lot of money.

2

They Don't Know
How to Do It

THE SECOND MOST COMMON REASON PEOPLE AT WORK DON'T do what they are supposed to do is, "They don't know how to do it." Frequently managers view this reason as similar to not knowing what they are supposed to do, but it is totally different. For example, I might know that I am supposed to motivate my office staff, but I don't know how to do it. So I scream and threaten. Is the following what your employees are saying to each other?

- O Whatever you do, don't tell the boss you don't know how to do something.
- O I know what I am doing is not the right way, but I don't know how else to do it.
- O If you don't know how to do it, fake it. They will never trace the error back to you.
- O When he asked if everyone knew how to do it, I raised my hand with all the rest; I didn't want to look like the only dummy in the group.

11

○ It doesn't do any good to ask her how to do it. When she tells you, she moves so fast and talks so fast you will still not know how to do it.

○ Every time you ask him for help, all you get is his big lecture on creativity and innovation.

Is the following what managers at your company say when their employees say, "I don't know how to do this?"

○ If I have to tell you how to do everything, what am I paying you for?

○ Can't you think for yourself?

○ I will be glad to help you with that, but I am just too busy right now.

○ Never mind. I will do it myself.

○ I explained how to do that once already. Do you want me to do your job for you?

○ We need people around here who can function independently.

○ Do I have to hold your hand on everything you do?

THE PROBLEM

Sometimes managers mistakenly assume that telling employees is teaching them. Telling is certainly an active part of teaching, although teaching can occur without telling. Demonstrating is one method of teaching without telling. But merely telling and demonstrating is not enough. For learning to occur, it is necessary for trainees to actually practice (simulate) doing the task being taught. If a supervisor only explains and demonstrates to a new sales clerk how to process a credit for returned merchandise without letting the clerk practice, the rest of the learning (practice) will occur in front of a customer. Mistakes made while practicing in front of customers are always more costly than mistakes made during practice (simulation) in training.

A common approach to training in business is to assign an experienced employee to teach a new employee how to do a job. Although the experienced person might be the best performer in that job, the big question is, "Does he or she know how to teach?" The answer, invariably, is "no." Teaching is not something you do naturally; it requires specific skills. If your experienced employee doesn't know how to teach, training may not be happening; therefore, your new employee may not be learning. Additionally, you probably don't test the new person to measure whether learning has occurred after the alleged training is finished. As a result, you think the new employee was taught by the experienced employee, but in reality, two people only shared some space and time.

One ineffective method of teaching when done by itself is the "monkey see, monkey do" approach. The trainer says, "See how I do it and you will see how you are supposed to do it." Unfortunately, when people who do things expertly use this method, they don't bother to describe all the little details of how or why they are doing what they do. As a result, there are some things the trainee does not see and more things he or she does not understand. The trainer will repeat the performance when the trainee doesn't seem to catch on the first time, but the trainee eventually becomes too embarrassed to say he or she still doesn't understand how to do it.

I know a woman whose first job after college graduation was as a software consultant to clients for a large computer company. When she told her boss that she did not know how to solve a client's software problem, his reply was, "I don't know either; fake it."

I have seen new production workers get five-minute instructions on a fast-moving production line and be told, "Now you do it and you will get the hang of it." The unfortunate worker is overwhelmed with the requirement to touch and assemble unfamiliar objects moving by rapidly.

I know of a saleswoman who, when promoted to sales trainer, was handed the sales training manual on Friday of her first week and told, "Read this over the weekend, because you are teaching the next sales trainee class on Monday." My sympathy went to the new salespeople who were doomed not to learn. Selling is one job; teaching selling is another job. Telling people to do something is definitely not teaching them how to do it.

Managers make too many assumptions about what people know without checking their assumptions. They promote the best accountant to accounting supervisor without providing any training in how to supervise people.

The three main reasons why employees don't know how to do what they are supposed to do are:

○ Managers assume the employees know how to do it

○ Managers really believe they are teaching when in fact they are only telling

○ Managers decide not to waste the time needed for teaching

Managers commonly want to minimize training time to get employees producing sooner. But managers don't realize that when people do not know how to do what they are supposed to do, they are receiving full pay while they give poor service or produce nonsalable and/or low-quality product, or they damage equipment and customer relationships—all contributing to higher costs.

PREVENTIVE SOLUTION

If you want people to know how to do what they are supposed to do, take the following steps:

1. Choose a single person to train new employees. Send the trainer to a seminar to learn teaching techniques.

2. Create a training manual for the instructor that will guide and standardize the training of new employees.

3. Provide detailed reference manuals for employees that will support learning and job performance after training. List the kinds of problems, along with the appropriate solutions, they could face when doing the job.

4. In all jobs where failure is important (including management jobs), give employees practice in

simulations of the actual work so they make their mistakes where the cost of failure to you and them is minimal. For example, if employees must use unfamiliar material, forms, and equipment or must act in unfamiliar ways, let them use those unfamiliar things initially in a nondistracting training environment.

5. Create a test for all new employees on a job so you will know whether learning has actually occurred. The test can be both written and actual performance. If new employees cannot pass the test, send them back for more training.

If you want to know whether employees know how to do something, don't ask, "Do you know how to do that?" If you get the answer "yes," you still don't know. Ask the employees to describe what it is they are going to do or give them a chance to demonstrate it while you watch.

3

They Don't Know What They Are Supposed to Do

AS AMAZING AS THIS MAY SOUND, THE MOST COMMON reason managers give as to why people at work don't do what they are supposed to do is, "They don't *know* what they are supposed to do." At its worst, this means literally that people do not know there is a specific task they should perform. Variations of this problem are:

○ They know they are supposed to do something, but they don't know when they are supposed to begin.

○ They know they are supposed to do something and know when they are supposed to begin, but they don't know when they are supposed to finish.

○ They know what to do, when to begin it, and when to end it, but they don't know what finished is supposed to look like. You told them to do a good job, but they don't know whether a good job is 10 percent error, 5 percent error, or error-free performance.

THE PROBLEM

An early warning of this problem is an employee's response to a boss's request with, "That's not my job." ·Managers usually interpret this response as poor attitude or lack of cooperation. But if what was requested is actually a part of that employee's job, why wouldn't they know that? The answer is, "We never told them; we were not specific enough." One manager told me that her boss used to tell her "Harriet, you have to hit the decks running." She said she never knew what he meant by that and was afraid to ask him.

Managers usually have an idea in their heads of what constitutes the job, but they don't completely describe that job to the person who must do it. So the employee has to guess a lot. Employees who don't know what they are supposed to do frequently do things they shouldn't be doing. This wastes the boss's time telling people, "Don't do that" or "You shouldn't be doing that."

There is a big discrepancy between what managers think is the employee's *responsibility* and what employees think they are supposed to *do*. What you are *responsible for* and what you *do* are two different subjects. The former is a general idea of accountability; the latter is an activity. You may be responsible for keeping your boss informed of problems, but were you told what is considered a problem or how soon you should communicate what you think

18

is a problem? Should you call your boss at home about a problem or should you wait for the regular staff meeting, and should you communicate it verbally in private or just include it in your monthly report?

One manager, when following up with his employee on a high-priority project he had labeled "ASAP" (As Soon As Possible), discovered that the work had not been done. When he asked, "Why didn't you do this as soon as possible, as I told you?" the worker's response was, "It hasn't been possible yet; I had other things to do." When the manager said, "Well, I labeled it ASAP because I wanted you to do that before everything else," the worker's answer was, "Why didn't you mark it 'BEE,' Before Everything Else?"

Managers complain that employees are late for work too frequently, but those same managers can't describe "allowable lateness." There are managers who complain that their sales representatives don't make enough sales calls, but the salespeople have not been told how many sales calls they should make per day, per week, or per month. There are managers who complain about other managers who don't respond soon enough to business problems, but no one has described how soon is "soon enough." There are maintenance supervisors who complain that their craft people don't perform maintenance tasks quickly enough. Yet the craft people are not told what the estimated task completion time should be, even on highly repetitive maintenance activities.

Every employee is responsible for being "on time for work"; unfortunately, "on time for work" is usually not described. Here are some employees' interpretations of "being on time" for a 9:00 a.m. start:

- Punching the time clock at 9:00 a.m.
- Walking toward your workstation or desk at 9:00 a.m.
- Hanging up your coat at 9:00 a.m.
- Getting a cup of coffee in the cafeteria at 9:00 a.m.
- Combing your hair in the rest room at 9:00 a.m.
- Leaving the locker room at 9:00 a.m.

Should the sales clerk be setting up merchandise on the counter at 9:00 a.m. or should that have been done before nine so customers could be served at nine?

This same ambiguity also occurs at the end of the day. Are you supposed to stop work at 5:00 p.m. and then clean up, or can you stop before five so the cleanup is finished by five? Without defining what to do, you may have:

- People sitting idly at their workstations already cleaned up waiting for the clock to strike five
- People standing at the exit before five waiting to run out to the parking lot at five o'clock
- People working overtime where overtime is not authorized
- People not working overtime although you consider that a natural part of the job

Many years ago, when I became the manager responsible for building security for a company, I was making the security rounds with a security guard to check the process. Along the way, the guard was describing to me what he was supposed to do. As we approached the warehouse overhead loading doors, he explained how important it was to make sure those doors were locked because of the high-value inventory in the warehouse. When I asked him how he did that, he said he looked at the two padlocks on the bottom of each door to be sure they were locked. When I asked him if he ever yanked on the padlocks to be sure they were actually locked, he said, "No, but that was a good idea." He bent down, yanked on the lock of the first door, and to his surprise, it came open. Mumbling his surprise, he proceeded to yank on the locks of the other doors. When he was finished, he said, "I am going to do that every time from now on."

I then asked him if he ever tried to raise an overhead door even though the locks were locked to make sure they would not open. He said no, he didn't think that was necessary, but if that was what I wanted, he would do it. He walked over to the next door, bent down to lift the door against the locks, and to his amazement, the door opened completely. After both of us recovered from shock, we discovered that the padlocks were locked but not engaged with the hasp on the floor. This was not the guard's fault; he was told what he was responsible for but not told what to do to meet that responsibility.

As another example, if you were my boss, you might have told me that I am responsible for maintaining an open door policy in my department. But you might not have told me that I must invite all of my employees into my office individually once each quarter to ask them about job problems, dissatisfactions, or for their suggestions how I or the company might help them perform better. And is it part of my job to observe employees daily at their work location to discover their problems, or am I supposed to wait for them to request my assistance?

There are managers who say, "Look into this problem for me," but they don't tell the employees when they should begin or end the task or whether they should take action to solve the problem or only produce a report describing it.

Knowledgeable teachers of management have said for years, "If you want to increase productivity, start with a good job description." Unfortunately, most job descriptions are written for the purpose of deciding what the job is worth rather than helping people know what they should do in that job. Responsibilities are generally described rather than job behaviors. Also, people rarely receive their own copy of the job description. It usually sits untouched on some shelf.

Companies do other weird things with job descriptions, such as restricting the job description to one page. This means that when you write a job description, if you haven't finished describing the job after one page, tough luck, the employee must guess the rest.

People seeking employment knock on a company's door saying, "I choose to give up doing what I would rather do in order to behave in a way for which you are willing to pay me." Management's response is, "That's fine, but we are not going to tell you exactly what it is you are supposed to do." As a result, most workers learn what they are supposed to do right by doing everything wrong at least once; everything left over is okay. This is a huge waste of time and money.

It's important to understand that the employment relationship is not slavery, serfdom, or human bondage; it is merely a behavior rental agreement.[1] Therefore, the job description must describe the behavior for which you pay the rent money. Behavior means the things a person must *do* to meet the responsibility of that job.

A lot of these behavior descriptions do exist in companies, but they are in procedure manuals, not in the job description. Procedure manuals describe exactly how the job should be done. If you had accurate job descriptions in your organization, you would need fewer procedure manuals.

Recently an administrative manager told me that although he is responsible for managing the manager of his company's cafeteria, he didn't know anything about managing restaurants and so he didn't know what information should be in the job description for that cafeteria manager. For example, he said that one of the responsibilities of the cafeteria manager was to provide an appetizing menu but he didn't know what that meant. After a lengthy discussion, we came up with the following:

An appetizing menu provides food that is purchased by the majority of the people served. Dissatisfaction with the menu would mean more than two complaints per day and/or more than 15 percent of any prepared appetizer or entree not being sold.

Those behaviors the cafeteria manager must *do* to meet his responsibility for maintaining appetizing menus are as follows:

- ○ Measure and record daily percent of unused appetizer and entree.
- ○ Prepare and conduct a written user survey once every three months.
- ○ Conduct verbal surveys by talking to a minimum of five cafeteria customers each day after they have dined to determine their satisfaction with both the food and the service.
- ○ Report (weekly) in writing to the administrative manager the current trends of cafeteria usage, complaints, and menu changes.
- ○ Change menus according to survey of usage data.
- ○ Present on one day each month one "special entree," representing a culinary specialty of one of the nations of the world.

You may think that these items are objectives as used in the Management by Objectives (MBO) process, but they are not. They are the normal required behaviors of the cafeteria manager's job. He will know he is supposed to do these things only if he is told to do them or if he dreams them up for himself. If failure is important to you, don't wait for him to finish dreaming.

Some managers avoid describing the job on purpose because they mistakenly believe it will give them more productivity. I've heard managers say, "If I don't tell them how much I want them to do, the chance is they will do more than I want." That certainly is a possibility, but is it a probability? The answer is "no."

Managers also reject this idea because they mistakenly believe that if you write down everything employees are supposed to do, you will stifle their creativity. This is nonsense; just because people know what they are supposed to do, they are not precluded from thinking up better ways of doing it. The real problem is that without complete job descriptions people waste their creativity inventing what everyone else knows they are supposed to do. Companies need to be creative in developing new products and services to ensure their future, but they will have no future if their employees don't do what they are supposed to do each day. Ninety percent of the jobs in our modern society don't require any creativity; they just need to be done correctly. Would you rather have people doing their jobs badly while inventing what they are supposed to do or have them perform perfectly with occasional new ideas about how it could be done better? The question is, "Are you hiring people to invent a job or are you hiring people to do a job your organization has already invented?"

More people at work will do what you expect if you tell them specifically what they are supposed to do, when to begin it, when to end it, and what finished is supposed to look like. Giving them vague instructions will get you vaguely related results.

PREVENTIVE SOLUTION

1. If the things your employees do are unimportant to you, if it doesn't matter when they begin

or end something or how they do it, let them do it any way they want to do it.

2. If you want to improve efficiency, and eliminate performance problems caused by your people not knowing what they are supposed to do, the solution is to tell them. Give them accurate job descriptions describing the job behaviors you pay for, the things you want them to do. View your job descriptions as behavior rental agreements.

3. If you want to know if your employees know what they are supposed to do, don't ask them if they know. If they say "yes," you will not be any wiser. Ask them to tell you what they are supposed to do.

4. When you describe a job, don't limit the number of pages of the job description. The number of pages is unimportant if your objective is to describe the complete job.

5. Don't assign this task of describing the job in behavioral terms to the personnel department. You, the manager, should do it in coordination with your subordinates. Discuss the employment relationship with your subordinates and define it so they recognize it is a behavior rental agreement. Then ask them to describe the things they think they must do on the job. The key word is "do." After you describe what you think the subordinate must do on the job, combine both lists to complete the behavioral list for the job description. The subordinates contribute their knowledge but don't vote on what is on the job description. This process is participative but not democratic. You are not asking them to

invent the job, you are merely asking them to help you define the job already invented. Once this task is completed, you don't have to repeat it unless aspects of the job change.

6. When assigning work projects, whether they be for one hour or one year, use the work planning approach: Mutually define the steps required to accomplish the project goal; then identify when each step should begin and end and how the ending of each step will be recognized if it is achieved.[2]

7. Don't worry about getting into too much detail. You will probably not get detailed enough. Besides, you cannot hurt job performance by describing everything that must be done. You can test this conclusion the next two times you eat in a restaurant. In the first restaurant be very non-specific in what you order and see what you are served to eat. In the second restaurant be very specific and see if the meal more closely approximates what you wanted compared to the first meal.

8. If you want more creativity, ask for it relative to specific problems and reward the effort. But caution your people that although you want ideas on how to do things better, it is necessary to evaluate and plan any changes to avoid unnecessary failures and to guarantee smooth teamwork.

4

They Think Your Way Will Not Work

WERE YOU EVER SHOWING ONE OF YOUR EMPLOYEES HOW TO do something your way when the response was:

- ○ "O.K., I'll try it, but I don't think it will work."
- ○ "Isn't this opening up a can of worms?"
- ○ "That is a nice idea in theory, but I have to operate in the real world around here."

Obviously, that employee thinks your way will not work. When employees think your way will not work, they have a logical reason for not doing it your way. This usually occurs as a problem when employees are new to the job or when you introduce a new approach or technique to someone who has performed that task for a long time.

THE PROBLEM

This problem does not refer to those rare situations when your way, in fact, will not work. If that were so, employees would be right in not doing it your way. It also does not refer to a task neither one of you knows how to do and your way may possibly not work. It refers to occasions when your way is effective, but your employees do not believe it. For example:

○ You tell your sales representative that he or she must close each sale by actually asking the customer to buy your products. But the representative says, "Asking customers to buy is backing them into a corner; it will make them angry and make it harder for me to see them in the future."

○ You tell your subordinate supervisor that if she verbally compliments an employee's small improvements in performance although performance is not yet up to standard, the employee's performance will most likely continue to improve. But she says, "Doing that is condoning substandard performance and will encourage employees to perform below standard."

○ You tell your credit supervisor that if he does not argue with complaining customers, they will calm down. But he says, "To do that is presenting a weak position and will encourage them to argue more."

○ You tell your technician that making detailed notes after each step in his experiments will not take much time and will provide a more accurate record. But his expressed point of view is, "Doing that will slow me down." So he makes inaccurate notes after the experiment is finished.

○ You tell your customer service clerk that the new computerized order entry system will speed up the total handling of all customer orders. He says, "It takes too much effort to enter the order, and the old system guarantees you never lose customer information."

PREVENTIVE SOLUTION

1. When you are trying to get employees to do things new to them, ask them to present their opinions about the task or project. If your employees really think it will not work, you want them to express that opinion so you can deal with it before the work begins.

2. The burden of responsibility is on you, the manager, to explain convincingly why your way will work. You are required to be convincing; merely telling them is not good enough. You have to sell them.

3. Preventing this problem with new employees is easier because what they think will not work is usually something your experienced employees have been doing successfully for some time. Simply present the proof that your way worked in the past. Preventing this problem with experienced employees who you want to do something differently may be more difficult. If "your way" has ever been successfully done before, you must present proof that it works. If it has never been done before, present the information you

have that leads you to expect it will work. In both situations, first explain in detail why it must be done your way and present your proof.

4. As a last resort, if you cannot convince your employees that your way will work, ask them to try it your way and announce that you will take full responsibility for the outcome. If the outcome is as successful as you expect, they will have proof that your way works. If you use this latter approach, however, be sure to watch their initial performance closely so employees don't deviate from your way—causing failure and then blaming your method for the failure.

5

They Think
Their Way Is Better

YOUR FIRST REACTION MIGHT BE THAT "THEY THINK THEIR way is better" is the same problem as the one discussed in the last chapter, but it is not. The emphasis here is on their way, not yours. They may think your way will work, but they think their way is better. In this situation, an employee might say, "I have always done it the other way," or, "Do we have to do everything your way?" or, "I think it is a waste of time to do it that way." Do these situations sound familiar?

○ Boss: Please check with the staff at each
critical point in your system design and get
approval before you proceed to your next step.
—Employee: I know exactly what they want. I
can save time by completing the system and
getting their approval at the end.

○ Boss: Please fill out your customer record after each sales call while the information is fresh.
—Employee: It is more convenient for me to fill out the customer records at the end of the day when I am not rushed.

○ Boss: Please use the safety guard when the machine is running.
—Employee: I am careful and can run the work faster without the safety guard.

○ Boss: Please give verbal recognition daily to your staff as you observe their achievements.
—Employee: I think they like it better when I send a memo to them every six months with a few "atta boys."

Here are some discussions managers have described to me:

○ Boss: You should not have run those want ads over the holidays. Didn't you know the response to employment advertising on holidays is very low?
—Employee: I thought a holiday would be a good time to run an ad because people would have plenty of time to read the newspapers.

○ Boss: You told me your accountant was a poor performer. Why did you give her a raise?
—Employee: I thought it would motivate her to perform better.

○ Boss: We can't collect payment from that customer. Why did you fill their order without prepayment?
—Employee: He said he really needed it, and I thought if we demonstrated some trust, he would feel obligated to pay.

○ Boss: The customer is angry because you told him we had it in stock but we don't. I told you to always check the physical inventory before making promises to customers.
  —Employee: I never thought that was necessary, I usually just check the inventory file and assume it's up to date.

○ Boss: The meeting leader is complaining because you set up the coffee service too late, which made the coffee break too long and put the meeting off schedule.
  —Employee: I usually set it up late so it will not interrupt their meeting.

○ Boss: We had to throw away another batch today because it did not meet the specifications. Did you measure each ingredient before you mixed it?
  —Employee: No, I thought I had a pretty good feel for the amounts required.

Frequently these situations are interpreted as simply resistance to change, but they are not. The employees are using logical thinking from their point of view. They may think your way will work, but they also think their way will work better. If employees really think their way is better, why in the world would they do it your way?

THE PROBLEM

Again, this does not refer to a situation where their way is better than yours. If that is true, they should do it their way and not your way. This situation refers to employees having misinformation about how successful their method is compared to your method.

Did you know that an occasional problem in selling pharmaceuticals to doctors is that some doctors, having used a certain drug on patients for many years, will not try a new drug because the old one has worked well for them so far? In that situation someone has failed to convince the doctor that the old drug is not as effective as the new one.

In almost all of my management seminars at least one manager will describe problem employees as those who don't think for themselves, always having to be told what to do. "Why can't they do things on their own? Why can't they be innovative?" managers say. Invariably, another manager in the same group will describe problem employees as those who don't do what you tell them to do. "They just can't seem to follow directions," the manager says.

Jokingly, I usually suggest that the two managers exchange employees. Unfortunately, that is really not the solution. Managers don't realize that employees who don't follow instructions may actually be thinking for themselves; they are being innovative. When employees think their way is better, they are in fact thinking for themselves. And frequently, they are doing what they think is in the best interest of the organization.

When employees choose an alternative different from the alternative you gave them and do the wrong things because they think their way is better, they are being innovative. But it is bad innovation. Bad innovation causes trouble for employees, you, your organization, and your customers.

Most managers like innovation or employees thinking for themselves as long as it works. When it fails, the manager's fallback position is, "Why can't they follow instructions?"

PREVENTIVE SOLUTION

1. Realize that innovation in a general sense is thinking of or trying to do things differently. You want to separate good innovation from bad innovation. Good innovation would be when employees think of, present, and try more effective ways of doing things that have a likelihood of success. Bad innovation would be when employees think of or try things that they think will work *but everyone else knows will not work.* In other words, if they knew what you know, they would have done it your way.

2. Before the work begins, discover whether this problem exists in any given situation. When planning a project or assigning a task, ask employees for their ideas and opinions about how it will be done. If they think their way is better, most employees will tell you that even without asking. But if you are in doubt about it, a good question to ask is, "Can you think of any reason why you might do this project differently than we have discussed?" You must uncover this reason before the work begins to prevent poor performance. Don't wait for it to cause a problem.

3. You, the manager, are responsible for convincingly presenting information that the employee's way is not better than the way it is supposed to be done. Telling is not enough. You have to sell to be convincing; the burden of proof is on you. One effective, convincing method is to explain in

detail the cause-effect relationship between the intended actions and the expected results. Then compare the difference in performance outcome or results between "your way" and "their way." This works almost all of the time.

4. Don't make the mistake of letting anyone do something wrong to prove you are right, especially if the cost of doing it the wrong way is high.

It is easy to be seduced by the idea that "people learn by experience." Learning by experience means that people will do things wrong until they discover there is a better way. But some people do a lot of things wrong before they get it right, some keep repeating the same wrong things, and some give up trying because they can't get it right. There is some truth in the idea that "people learn by failing," but it is even more true that people learn by succeeding. If you were an animal living alone in the wilderness, you would have to go through a lot of trial and error to survive, and you might not make it in one piece. As intelligent human beings, we are able to follow a more sophisticated rule about experience, which is, "Learn from other people's experience." That way we can avoid doing all the dumb things other people thought were good ideas at the time and learn more in less time while suffering fewer bumps and bruises.

Doing things wrong wastes time and materials, loses customers, is embarrassing, and sometimes injures people. It is more beneficial for both of you to get the employee to do it your way.

5. As a last resort, if all of your convincing efforts fail, ask, "Is there anything I can do to convince you that your way is not better than my way?" If their answer is "no," tell them the discussion is ended and the project must be done your way.

6

They Think
Something Else
Is More Important

MANAGERS INITIALLY DESCRIBE THIS REASON FOR NONPERFOR-
mance as "The employee doesn't have enough time."
When I ask managers if they mean the employee is
asked to do more than he can do in the time available, they answer, "No, he is merely doing something
else of a lower priority." When I ask why this is happening, the answer is usually, "Well, the employee
thinks the other item is of a higher priority." In other
words, *the employee thinks something else is more
important*.

THE PROBLEM

You will know you have this problem when an
employee gives you one of these reasons for nonperformance:

○ I haven't had time to get to it yet

○ I didn't know you were in a big rush for it

○ I had a few other things to take care of

○ That will be the next thing on my list

○ I can do only one thing at a time

These answers sound like excuses, but your employee merely thought something else was of a higher priority. Usually when you are confronted with a priority problem, the situation is merely that someone thinks something else is more important. As simple as this sounds, it is frequently true that some employees do not really know the comparable priority of the many tasks and projects assigned to them. This usually happens because:

○ The boss does not assign priorities to tasks

○ The boss labels all tasks number one priority

○ The boss changes the priority without informing the employee

○ The priorities of the employee's multiple projects/tasks change as the work mix changes and the formula for deciding what is more important at any moment has not been explained to the employee.

For the most part, this problem is not that employees are not working. They are simply working on what they think is important in contrast to what the manager thinks is important. For example:

○ The accounting clerk who thinks it is more important to be perfect than to finish on time

○ The shipping clerk who thinks it is more important to finish on time than to be accurate

- The engineer who thinks it is more important to search for all the possible data than to keep the project on schedule

- The chemist who thinks it is more important to work on her pet project than to work on what supports the project team

- The manager who thinks it is more important to be liked by subordinates than to correct their policy and rule violations

- The credit manager who thinks it is more important to crack down on marginal credit risks than to support increased sales

Of course, there are those situations when the important things from the employee's point of view are way out of balance. For example:

- The executive who thinks it is more important to hold surprise staff meetings at his/her convenience than to use advanced planning to avoid disruption in the tightly scheduled activities of the staff

- The systems analyst who thinks it is more important to defend her image than to admit she made a mistake

- The sales clerk who thinks it is more important to have a stunning appearance than to be on time

- The technician who thinks it is more important to appear competent than to admit not knowing something

- The clerk who thinks it is more important to complete lunchtime shopping than to be back to work on time

○ The employee who thinks it is more important to be out of the parking lot first than to complete the last hour of the workday

Sometimes managers introduce high-priority projects to subordinates with careful and dramatic emphasis, but when the priorities change, the change is communicated as incidental information.

A manager in the research department for an international chemical company recently told me that he and his staff had been picked as a task force to work on a two-year project that was described as having utmost and primary importance to the future destiny of the corporation. He told me that five corporate executives met with his staff in an all-day meeting to stress the importance of that project. Six months later the same research staff was invited to another meeting conducted by one corporate executive who announced that the corporation decided to change direction. A new long-range project was presented and identified as being of utmost and primary importance to the future destiny of the corporation, and the previously assigned projects should be disregarded. This second meeting lasted one hour. The research manager told me that he had difficulty getting his employees to stop working on the first project.

There is a limited amount of time in any workday. If your employees spend that time working on unimportant things, you and your organization are in trouble. Sometimes the only difference between a successful and an unsuccessful organization is that the employees in the successful organization are working on the right things. The employees in the unsuccessful organization are working, but they are working on the wrong things, what they think is important.

PREVENTIVE SOLUTION

1. If the work you assign to your employees is of multiple priorities or the priorities change frequently, label the work according to its priority when you assign it. Explain to employees in detail why one task is a higher priority over another.

2. If the work they do comes from some other source, give your employees a list of priority categories so they can prioritize the work when they receive it.

3. If the priority of employees' work changes based on changing factors in their work situation, give them the same formula you use to distinguish the most important work from the less important work at any moment in time.

4. When work priorities change, let the employees be the first ones to know of the change rather than the last ones to know.

5. If you frequently change what you identify as "hot priorities," you must devote sufficient communication time and effort at the time of change to make certain everyone understands which project is *now* the "hot project" and why it is so.

6. If you now label everything a "hot project," stop that foolishness. Even in hospital emergency rooms some emergencies have higher priority

over other emergencies. Maintaining constant panic situations in the work environment is not productive. People respond to situations of continuous panic by slowing down and doing what they can reasonably do, or they leave your organization.

7

There Is No
Positive Consequence
to Them for Doing It

A LOT OF MANAGERS CONSIDER THE LAST POSSIBLE REASON FOR nonperformance to be "There is no positive consequence to them" because they simply don't understand what a positive consequence is from the employee's point of view or how rewards affect performance.

Look at the situations listed here and ask yourself, from the performer's point of view, whether the consequences of these actions are rewarding.

○ I worked late last night to finish a report, but when I gave it to my boss this morning, she didn't even look up from her desk.

○ Six months ago I gave my boss a suggestion for improving the process, and I haven't heard anything from him since then.

○ I am trying to find the bugs in this program, but I am making no headway.

○ After my boss told me that bringing up unrelated material at staff meetings was making the meetings excessively long, I stopped doing that, but he said nothing to me afterward.

○ When I told my boss that we were going to complete the project on schedule, she said, "You don't get medals for doing what you are paid to do."

○ Since my boss warned me about shortages, I make a special effort so my cash drawer balances each day, but my boss never says anything to me about it.

THE PROBLEM

Obviously, there is an absence of positive consequence or reward to the performer in each of these instances. But many managers would say that getting paid for doing those things is the reward. Unfortunately, it doesn't work that way. According to human behavior research, the weekly paycheck does not qualify as a reward that influences people's productivity. The psychologist B.F. Skinner once observed, "People don't come to work to get paid, they come to work so the pay doesn't stop." Additionally, in most business organizations, an employee can perform badly for a long period of time before the pay stops. Getting a weekly paycheck is like breathing; it only becomes important when it stops.

Human behavior research indicates that people do things for which they are rewarded and, conversely, do not do those things for which they are not rewarded. In other words, performance that is rewarded will increase in its frequency; the reward reinforces the good performance. Rewards can be separated into two categories: those externally delivered from someone else and those internally delivered by the person performing. The external rewards can be further separated as either tangible, such as jelly beans, a trophy, or money, or intangible, such as a verbal compliment, an expression of appreciation, or even a smile. All internal rewards are intangible, in that people talk to themselves about achieving a symbolic goal or status, such as:

○ "I am an honest person."
○ "I am a kind person."
○ "I am a hard worker."
○ "I am doing that task better than I used to do it."
○ "I am working less and getting away with it."

Research also suggests that these positive consequences or rewards, whether they be internal, external, tangible, or intangible, are most effective when they occur immediately following the specific action being rewarded and when the reward occurs at a high frequency. In other words, small awards received immediately and frequently seem to have more effect on performance than larger rewards delivered long after performance and infrequently. The only reward managers control that meets these high-frequency requirements is the manager's specific verbal compliments about performance. These compliments can be delivered at a high frequency, immediately following performance, and are very inexpensive. Unfortunately, they rarely occur by the hour or by the day in the normal workplace.

Some managers don't bother to verbally reward employee performance because they think compliments have no value. These managers don't realize that merely having the title makes each of them a *significant other* in the lives of his or her employees. "Significant other" is a clinical term used to identify the relative importance of one person in another person's life. Acceptance or rejection of a person from the significant other has a lot more value than the same response from anyone else. So your verbal or e-mail compliments about performance do influence performance.

Many managers tell me, "I send memos to my employees complimenting them on good performance; isn't that a positive consequence?" "Yes," I answer, "but how many memos can you send a single employee each day?" "Well, you don't," they reply. "You can only do that three or four times a year." That is the problem with memos: you can't deliver them frequently enough. If high frequency is the rule, verbal compliments win over memos. "But," they say, "if you asked an employee whether they would rather receive a memo or a ten-second compliment, they would all choose the memo." I agree that they would all choose the memo, but we are not talking about what kind of reward employees would rather receive, we are talking about the delivery system that has the most effect on performance, and high frequency is more effective.

Analysis of the work environment reveals that employees' rewards come from only three sources: the work itself, fellow employees, and the boss.

An example of rewards from the work itself would be when you polish your car. As the shine shows through the dirt and grime as you polish, you are rewarded for your polishing action. When you are finished, you might even say to yourself, "Gee, that looks great." The same kind of positive consequence can occur when computing figures, or during problem analysis, or when creating reports, or when repairing something. If the job is serving customers, it can be a comment of satisfaction by the customer.

An example of rewards from fellow employees would be your neighbor telling you what a nice polishing job you did on your car, such as, "Hey, that looks great; I wish I had the patience to do mine." Unfortunately, it is not common for employees to compliment fellow employees on their good work. Compliments are usually about avoiding work, such as, "I wish I was like you and didn't worry about the errors," or "I wish I could ignore weekly reports like you do," or "I envy your control; no matter how hectic things get around here, you just chug along at your own pace."

The third source is the boss's positive comments about performance, such as, "Thanks for putting in the extra time on that report," or "I know your project is not working out yet, but I appreciate that you are still trying," or "Thanks for restricting your comments to the meeting agenda."

Many tasks or entire jobs are difficult to do, are repetitive, boring, or even unpleasant to do. In such a situation, if the employees do not view their work as rewarding and the manager does not deliver rewards for the work activity, there is most likely no positive consequence to them for doing it.

51

One primary reason why managers do not use verbal compliments to manage performance is because of the ridiculous reasoning, "I pay them for doing that and they are supposed to do it, so why should I compliment them for doing it?" The answer is, "If you don't compliment them for doing it to reinforce it, they may not continue to do it even though you pay them for it." Managers should realize that rewarding employees for appropriate performance is a *performance maintenance* intervention. It helps you get what you pay for.

PREVENTIVE SOLUTION

1. You must deliver "rewards" as reinforcers for the performance you expect and pay for. Use verbal rewards describing specific performance as soon as possible after performance occurs to maintain the desired performance. To be able to do that, you must get out from behind your desk and look for achievements. Since most of the people working for you do at least 90 percent of the things they are supposed to be doing, it should be easy to catch them doing something right.

   Here are some examples of rewarding performance:

   ○ I noticed you put in some extra time last night to complete this report on time; I really appreciate your effort.
   ○ Thank you for your suggestion for improving the process; that is the kind of teamwork that will help us succeed. I will get back to you as soon as we evaluate your suggestion.

○ I want to compliment you on your persis-
tence. I notice that you are continuing to
search for the bugs in that program. Keep up
your effort and you will eventually succeed.
○ Thank you for limiting your discussion to
the agenda material in today's staff meeting
like I asked you to. Your cooperation helped
the meeting go faster.
○ Another job well done. You certainly work
hard to keep us on schedule; keep up the
good work.
○ Since I mentioned the problem to you, you
are doing a good job balancing out your cash
and receipts each day. Thanks for your
attention to detail.

2. When verbally rewarding subordinates, do it pri-
vately to avoid "apple polisher" comments (negative consequences) from fellow workers.

3. Your verbal compliments should be specific
about the things done; avoid the generalizations,
such as "good job," "terrific," and "atta boy."

4. If you take the time to ask people to improve
their performance, you must take the time to
check for improvement and verbally compliment any improvement. E-mail is good for
quickly rewarding performance but not good for
finding out what is happening because it generally avoids the give-and-take of a direct conver-
sation which can pursue detailed information.

5. If someone gives you a five-part report on time
but Section Four is inappropriate, separate the
good from the bad in your comments. You might
say, "Thanks for getting your report in on time.
Sections One, Two, Three, and Five are exactly

what we need. Let's talk about changes you can make to Section Four which will bring it up to the professional level of the rest of your report."

6. Don't wait for people to complete projects before you deliver positive consequences. Compliment them for doing the right things which will lead to completed projects. This is one way of managing performance to guarantee the end result.

7. Here are some examples of tangible rewards:
   ○ You did such a great job on that difficult report, here is an easy one.
   ○ You take so much effort to make your work accurate, I thought you should have the first new computer.
   ○ You work so hard and succeed so well at meeting our deadlines, I would like to buy lunch for you today.
   ○ You are one of the few people with 100 percent attendance. Why don't you leave twenty minutes early tomorrow to start the weekend?

Other tangible rewards are bonus and commission payments, but these are more effective when paid at a high frequency. For example, a monthly sales bonus has more influence on improving sales performance than an annual bonus. Small awards for monthly perfect attendance have more influence on improving yearly attendance than annual awards for perfect attendance. Some companies arrange for managers to be able to distribute $100 per month in $5 to $20 amounts as rewards to employees for accomplishments during the month when they occur.

Once you think about it, you will create your own larger list of tangible rewards and inexpensive verbal rewards. But please remember that the verbal compliments about work well done are the least expensive and are highly effective.

If your employees work at home or in the field and you observe their performance infrequently, you will not have enough information about what they are *doing* to catch them doing something right. Your only solution is to get out there and observe their performance more frequently and spend more time on the phone while they tell you what they are doing. If you can't do that, you can't manage their performance, so treat them like independent contractors and pay only for results.

8

They Think
They Are Doing It

HAVE YOU EVER TOLD EMPLOYEES ABOUT A PROBLEM WITH their performance and they were surprised to hear that they had done something wrong? When you told them they did something wrong, did they say, "It looked okay to me"? If so, you have encountered this common problem. Those employees were not doing what they were supposed to be doing because they thought they were doing what they were supposed to be doing. This is not double-talk; the problem is inadequate feedback to the performers; they don't know they are failing. If you asked your employees, "How do you know when you are doing a good job?" would you get answers that sound like this:

○ When you leave me alone, I know I am doing a good job.

○ We must be doing okay because there have not been any speeches about quality lately.

○ I must be doing okay because you always tell me when we make too many errors.

○ When I get a pain over my left eye, I know I'm doing a good job.

○ When you don't send my reports back, I know I'm doing a good job.

○ When you don't glare at me in meetings, I know I'm doing a good job.

○ When I feel comfortable doing it, I know I'm doing a good job.

THE PROBLEM

Obviously these employees are not getting enough feedback about their work. And if these really were answers from your employees, their work performance is not as good as it could be.

One of the things you don't read about in most management books is how important feedback is as an influence on performance. All psychologists agree that feedback is one of the most critical requirements for sustained high-level performance of any human act. Feedback is the individual or collective signals (what you see, hear, smell, and feel) that tell you how you are doing. Without appropriate feedback, you could be doing something much worse or much better than you think. If employees think they are performing okay, they have no reason to change.

Managers usually understand their own need for feedback; they want to know how their department is doing against goals, budgets, and other performance indices and frequently record performance by the month, the week, the day, or the hour. Unfortunately, managers rarely give that information to subordinates as feedback until weeks or months later, or only when a problem occurs and it is too late to change performance. Telling employees this month their performance was good or bad on the first Tuesday of last month has no effect on that performance. The feedback may be specific, but it is too late.

If the objective is to achieve perfect performance, the timing of feedback is essential. Picture yourself about to get into your locked car. You reach into your pocket for your car keys, but they are not there. You peer through your car window to discover the car keys are in the ignition. That feedback about the whereabouts of your car keys is specific but too late. Getting feedback about the location of the car keys when you were about to lock the car door would have been more timely feedback. Fortunately, modern automobiles provide that kind of feedback with a bell or buzzer. When you open your car door while the key is in the ignition but the motor is not running, you get the signal. It is timely feedback, but not too specific. The bell or buzzer just signals you that something is wrong; it doesn't tell you specifically whether your lights are on, or your brakes are not on, or your keys are in the ignition.

Feedback to an employee that a mistake has been made is not as helpful as feedback that a mistake is about to be made. In the first instance, the deed is done and wasted. In the second instance, the deed can be modified to be done correctly. Telling your employee that a report has been completed incorrectly is late feedback. If instead you follow up and check the employee's work before the report is finished, you can give feedback that will modify the work and prevent a report from being completed incorrectly. Yet most of the feedback to employees is too late and negative, such as:

- ○ "That's not what I want."
- ○ "That is not up to our professional standard."
- ○ "You have too much data."
- ○ "You don't have enough data."
- ○ "This work is unacceptable."
- ○ "You are falling behind."

Giving nonspecific feedback, whether positive or negative, is another big feedback problem. Telling employees, "You are not cutting the mustard," or "You are not tuned in," is not specific enough to improve performance. Telling employees, "Your performance is dynamite," or "You are getting your act together," also does not communicate helpful information; the feedback is positive but too general. Even well-intentioned feedback can cause you problems if it is not done correctly. Psychologists are now reporting that people with unrealistically high opinions of themselves become quite aggressive when confronted with criticism and can become violent. This is a good reason to target behavior, not the person.

Many companies rely on the annual performance appraisal discussion to give feedback to employees about their performance with the assumption that it will improve performance. Unfortunately, this annual feedback is invariably not specific enough, is too late, and definitely is not frequent enough to improve performance. In fact, it is difficult to find anything you can do as a manager once a year that will have a lasting effect on employee performance. You can do things to influence their performance, but the effect is only temporary.

PREVENTIVE SOLUTION

1. A good example of how most companies use feedback effectively is during their employee community fund-raising drives. Management communicates the progress toward goals by day, by unit, and by department. This feedback is posted on bulletin boards, in newsletters, in paycheck envelopes, and on colorful signs around the office, at employee entrances, and in the cafeteria showing daily and weekly progress. That is a good example of how you should be giving feedback to your employees about your organization's performance.

2. Feedback can be positive, negative, or neutral and can be general or specific. Here are some examples of these different kinds of verbal feedback:

   ○ *Situation:* Frank Gruff, one of your new department managers, usually interrupts people when they are expressing their ideas in staff meetings.
   Feedback—general, negative: "Frank, you are an insensitive person; you are ruffling people's feathers."
   Feedback—specific, neutral: "Frank, I noticed in the last few staff meetings that you frequently interrupt people when they are presenting their views. I received four complaints about that in the last month."

○ *Situation:* At the next staff meeting Frank interrupts no one.
Feedback—general, positive: "Frank, I see you got the message—keep those horns tucked in."
Feedback—specific, positive: "Frank, you didn't interrupt anyone in today's meeting; that helped the meeting go more smoothly. Thanks for your cooperation."

○ *Situation:* You are playing golf with a friend who lifts his head on three out of five strokes off the tee.
Feedback—specific, negative: "You still lift your head on your tee shots like a novice golfer. Don't worry about losing your ball; you never hit it that far."
Feedback—specific, neutral: "I don't know if you are aware of this, but did you know that you lift your head on three out of every five tee shots?"
Feedback—specific, positive: "Since I mentioned your head lifting on your tee shots, you have improved by 80 percent. If you concentrate on that like you did on your grip problem, you will really improve your ball control."

○ *Situation:* Charlie Swift runs his machine too fast, causing excessive vibrations and wear on the equipment.
Feedback—general, negative: "Charlie, you are screwing up our equipment."
Feedback—specific, neutral: "Charlie, you are running your machine faster than the recommended operating speed, which causes excessive vibration and wear."

○ *Situation:* One hour later you notice that Charlie is running his machine slower but it is still too fast.

Feedback—general, negative: "Charlie, you are still screwing up our equipment."
Feedback—specific, positive: "Charlie, I see you have slowed your machine down, reducing vibration. If you reduce the RPM's a little bit more, you will eliminate the vibration altogether. Thanks for your cooperation."

3. Providing feedback in work situations where there has been little feedback increases productivity dramatically without making any other change. Feedback throughout the day will improve total performance for that day. Feedback at the end of the day is only a score for that day and has no impact on that day's performance (output).

4. As the boss, you should give verbal, positive, specific feedback several times per day.

5. If your organization keeps track of the quantity and quality of what people do by the hour or by the day, find a way of communicating that to them as simply as possible by the hour or by the day in their work area. Put up blackboards or electronic scoreboards in work areas where supervisors can display performance quantity and quality figures in large letters two to six times per day so employees can see how they are doing throughout the day.

6. Record achievement rates, not failure rates. Don't record 10 percent errors, record 90 percent perfect. Managers have told me that merely changing reports to reflect achievements rather than failures has resulted in higher achievement numbers.

7. As much as possible, ask employees to record their own feedback by keeping score on how

they do by hour or by day. Give them forms or counters to help them.

8. If you have to give feedback to employees about poor performance, make it specific and neutral. Talk about the performance, not the person.

9

They Are Rewarded for Not Doing It

WHAT MANAGER IN HIS RIGHT MIND WOULD REWARD employees for performing badly? The answer is that most managers do it daily as an unconscious act. Here are a few examples:

○ Employees who do difficult tasks poorly are given only easy tasks to perform.

○ Employees who are difficult to control receive job assignments giving them a lot of freedom.

○ Employees who repeatedly complain to the boss about certain work assignments are given those work assignments less frequently.

○ Employees who perform badly receive a lot of attention from the boss, who plays amateur psychologist and buys them coffee or lunch.

○ When employees make errors in their work, the boss corrects the errors.

THE PROBLEM

When a manager is asked to send a representative to a company activity, on company time, at company expense, who is frequently sent—the good worker or the bad worker? The manager sends the only employee he can afford to lose—the bad worker.

When a department manager is asked to recommend someone for promotion, frequently a bad employee is recommended, rather than a good employee, because the manager cannot run the department without the good performer.

I know of one company that defuses its union problems by promoting the troublesome union representative to supervisory status, thereby removing the troublemaker from the opposition ranks. In that company, if you want to be a supervisor, just become a union representative and then make a lot of anti-management noise.

Sometimes managers tell me that the reason why employees don't do what they are supposed to do is because of personality conflict: they don't like the boss. When I ask, "If an employee does not like the boss, what does he gain by not doing what he is supposed to do?" the answer is, "He hurts the boss." In some work situations, the only fun part of the day is to see how many times the employees can cause the boss to lose control. If causing pain to the boss is the only reward for your employee on the job, your days at work will be miserable.

A rule of human behavior mentioned in a previous chapter is that performance which is rewarded will increase in its frequency. This rule works whether or not the behavior is desirable. This means that if you repeatedly reward your subordinates' complaining behavior with your *attention,* complaining behavior will increase in frequency. Your *intentions* are not important; it is your *attention* that is the rewarding consequence.

You should consider the possibility that you may be intervening as a manager in ways that influence your employees to perform poorly, and you don't even know you are doing it.

PREVENTIVE SOLUTION

1. The first step is to analyze the consequences you deliver when employees fail or cause you problems. From the employees' point of view, is what you do a reward to them?

2. Do not reward employees for nonperformance. Stop buying coffee and lunch for bad performers. Don't play amateur psychologist; keep your discussions related to performance.

3. When employees make errors, require them to correct the errors. Assist as necessary, but don't correct the errors yourself.

4. Reward employees for the opposite of what you don't want. In other words, give them your attention for doing things you want them to do. For example, compliment them for being 10 minutes late when it happens as an improvement versus only talking to them when they are 20 minutes late. Say, "I see you have cut your lateness problem by 50 percent. Keep up the effort and you will be on time."

5. When employees do a difficult task poorly, manage them closely to eliminate the other possible reasons for nonperformance. But keep assigning the difficult task until performance improves or you remove these employees from the job requiring that task.

6. When employees are difficult to control, apply the necessary management control and/or deliver negative consequences to them for poor performance, such as progressive discipline. But be quick to verbally reward improvements if performance gets better after formal discipline.

7. When employees complain *repeatedly* about a work assignment that is assigned fairly and is unavoidable, ignore the complaints. Give verbal rewards, however, when the work assignment is performed correctly.

8. When talking to employees who perform badly, restrict your discussion to the reasons for nonperformance outlined in this book. Hold your discussion in the work area (in private) and don't buy them lunch or coffee during these discussions. When performance improves, you can compliment employees, talk about their outside interests, and buy them coffee or lunch.

9. If you conclude that employees are out to hurt you, do three things:

    a. Don't show the pain—don't rant and rave, showing you've lost control (and they have scored a point).
    b. Concentrate on giving employees verbal compliments when they do anything right.

c. Try to make friends with these employees, talk about personal things—show a personal interest, smile at them; try to find out why they are trying to hurt you. It's okay to say, "I get the feeling you don't like me and I don't know why. Can you tell me why?"

10

They Are Punished
for Doing
What They Are
Supposed to Do

DID ONE OF YOUR EMPLOYEES EVER APPROACH YOU DURING
your hectic, busy, demanding day to announce a
problem or request your help and your response was,
"What have you people screwed up this time?" or
"Can't you do anything for yourself?" or "Do I have to
do everything for you?" These are good examples of
shooting the messenger who delivers the bad news.

Human behavior research shows that when people
do things that are followed by punishment, they tend
to do those things less frequently. In the above
instances, the employee who approached the boss in
the interest of the organization was punished for that
approach. Here are more examples of punishment
following appropriate performance:

O The employee who does difficult work well is
assigned all of the difficult work.

○ The employee who makes suggestions at meetings gets to do extra projects to carry out the suggestions.

○ The employee who tries to be innovative hears the boss yelling, "Why can't you follow instructions like everyone else?"

○ The employee who attempts to do something for the first time and fails is faced with the inherent punishment of failure.

○ The employee who comes early and stays late is called an eager beaver by fellow workers.

○ The employee sweeping up his work area is told by the boss that he is finally doing work that fits his personal qualifications.

○ The employee who regularly calls the boss from the field as instructed always gets yelled at by the boss for something.

THE PROBLEM

Notice that all punishment does not come solely from the boss. Some punishment is intrinsic in the job, such as attempts followed by failure, and some punishment comes from fellow workers. Also note that in some of the examples, if the behavior preceding the punishment had not occurred, the punishment would not have been delivered. If the employee didn't call the boss as required, the boss would not yell at the employee. Being ridiculed by the boss when announcing problems can be avoided by not announcing problems. The chilling observation here is that people working for you can avoid punishment by not doing some of the things you want them to do. You would be correct in concluding that if you continued to deliver punishment in these situations, you would be managing employees to not do what you want them to do.

This problem is worse than it would appear on the surface. A good example is company sick pay policies that punish people for not using paid sick days. A recent survey of how 80 companies were dealing with high-cost absenteeism revealed that almost 50 percent of the companies that paid people for sick days would not let employees accumulate unused sick days. For example, if six sick days were allowed per employee per year and they were not used, those six days would be lost to the employee. Forget the philosophical discussions about what really is a sick day and why it should not be used unless there really is illness. What it really means from the employee's point of view is, "The company is willing to pay me for six nonworking days, and if I don't use them, I will lose them."

The vice president of sales for one company was lamenting to me that very few of his 700 salespeople ever had two consecutive years of sales growth; each individual's high-performance sales year was preceded by a low-performance year. After a brief analysis, I pointed out to him that the company paid sales bonuses based on the percentage of sales improvement or growth over the previous year. Since it was difficult for salespeople to sustain a large percentage of sales growth year after year, they adopted the strategy of planning a bad year so they could follow it with a good year. It was common for salespeople to be heard saying, "This is my year to hold back." These are examples of companies designing people management systems without a complete understanding of what influences people's behavior.

Sometimes managers tell me the reason why employees don't do what they are supposed to do is that the employees think the job is beneath them. When I ask the managers what they mean by that, they say, "The employees think they are capable of doing more important, more difficult, or more complicated work. They think what they are doing is below their skill or intelligence level."

"That does not make any sense," I reply. "Having higher-level knowledge or skill does not prevent someone from doing something requiring less skill or intelligence. If you were an automotive engineer, that would not automatically preclude you from properly changing a flat tire on your car."

"No," they say, "the problem is that the automotive engineer feels that changing tires all day long as a job is beneath him and perhaps embarrassing or even degrading."

"Now you've got it," I say. "When you ask people to do jobs that they interpret as beneath them and embarrassing and perhaps degrading, there is in their mind a negative consequence to them for doing it."

The negative consequence may only be in their heads, but it nevertheless is a negative consequence to them. This situation is made worse when snide remarks and sarcasm are received from fellow employees. In some companies the production or warehouse employees don't go to the personnel department for assistance when they need it because, as they say, "I feel like such a slob when I walk into the front office in my dirty work clothes."

In a large clerical department of one insurance company, the employees don't approach the manager with problems or suggestions because it is too punishing. Anyone who approaches the manager's office more than once every two weeks must walk a gauntlet of fellow workers making kissing sounds.

In a lot of organizations nonparticipation at staff meetings is the result of punishment delivered by peers after each staff meeting to individuals who have not yet learned the informal rules about "teamwork," "one hand washes the other," or "don't make us look bad in staff meetings."

In some companies it is a management development practice for selected junior-level managers to make verbal presentations at the monthly executive staff meetings. Although this practice is touted as beneficial to the junior managers and an opportunity to build their future, a junior manager will do anything to avoid doing it. The reason for this avoidance becomes clear once the actual meeting is observed. It seems that such a presentation is the only point in the monthly meeting when the executives have fun. They try to outdo each other in badgering, confusing, and belittling the presenter and afterward over lunch have a lot of laughs over how destructive they were.

Managers who are yellers and screamers have told me, "I don't mean to punish them, it is just my way." The sad truth is that if an employee is punished for doing something, the manager's *intentions* are irrelevant; the *consequence* that lands on the employee is what will influence future performance.

PREVENTIVE SOLUTION

1. To eliminate this reason for your employees not doing what they are supposed to be doing you have two alternatives: remove the punishment, or provide a reward to balance out the punishment.

2. To remove the punishment, change your behaviors that actually deliver punishment, as follows:

   a. When employees send you reports, don't return them with only negative comments; include good comments.

   b. When employees contact you voluntarily for some reason, make sure you don't use that situation to chew them out about something else. Save that until later.

   c. Keep a record of your interactions with employees and classify each one as either positive or negative from the employee's point of view. Make sure that at least half of the interactions are positive or at least neutral for the employee.

   d. When employees come to you with problems or ask for help, thank them specifically for doing that and explain how that really helps improve your organization's teamwork. Then give them the required help.

   e. Eliminate sarcasm from your workplace. When employee participation during meetings is followed by sarcasm and sniping from other meeting participants, you, as the meeting leader, must announce that is not allowed.

   f. Review your company policies and interpret them from the employee's point of view. Change policies that punish employees for doing what you want them to do. For example, let employees accumulate unused sick days forever.

3. Provide a reward to balance the punishment in those situations where the work is intrinsically punishing, as follows:

   a. When an unpleasant job that is intrinsically punishing must be done, balance the negative consequence by delivering a positive consequence for doing that job, such as extra compliments or even extra free time.

   b. When employees do difficult work well, reward them by giving them easy work to do before assigning more difficult work again. In other words, change the sequence of events; unpleasant work should be followed by pleasant work followed by unpleasant work.

   c. When employees are punished by fellow workers for doing what they are supposed to do, you must deliver rewards to balance out that situation. For example, when an employee receives only sarcastic comments from fellow workers for doing certain tasks, such as "cleanup," you, the boss, can counterbalance the punishment by giving compliments in private for doing those same tasks.

   d. If you must ask employees to do something they think is beneath them, explain why the work or project must be done, how important it is, and why they are being asked to do it and follow up with "a" and "b."

11

They Anticipate
a Negative Consequence
for Doing It

"ANTICIPATING A NEGATIVE CONSEQUENCE FOR AN ACTION" IS
not the same as the last reason, in which there actually was a negative consequence to employees for
doing what they were supposed to do. This reason
occurs when employees *think* there will be a negative
consequence to them for performing appropriately,
but there is none. Managers initially state this reason
for nonperformance as, "They think they can't do it,"
or "They don't have confidence," or "They are afraid."
After much discussion, the managers realize that
these all relate to the employee's anticipation of a
future undesirable or unpleasant outcome for performing. In other words, fear is the anticipation of a
negative consequence. At times, people don't do
what they are supposed to do because they anticipate
a negative consequence to themselves if they do it.

THE PROBLEM

An interesting aspect of this problem is that the anticipated negative consequence does not really have to be there for a person to have that fear. If employees think a negative consequence will occur, that is enough; it is a reality from their point of view. Another interesting aspect of fear is that fear does not incapacitate everyone. Think of all the things you did in your life even though you were afraid to do them.

The following are statements commonly heard at all levels in organizations describing anticipation of a negative consequence.

- I was afraid to ask you a question in the seminar because I thought it might be a dumb question.
- I was afraid to tell you I didn't know how to do it because you might think I am too stupid to do the job.
- I didn't bring up my idea at the meeting because I thought the rest of the group might think it presumptuous of me as a new member.
- I didn't tell him that being one day late with his report was better than being five days late because he might think it was okay to be one day late.
- I was afraid to tell the boss that he didn't have the right to yell and verbally abuse me because I thought I might lose my job.
- I was afraid to disagree with the rest of the executives because they might think of me as a non-team player.

○ I was afraid to try what I thought was a better way because if it didn't work I would really be in trouble.

○ I was afraid to go over my boss's head to complain about the unfair performance appraisal because I thought it would hurt my future.

Unfortunately, your employees may not express their fears to you. Employees who are afraid of you might not voluntarily talk to you; if they talk to you, they may not tell you the truth, may not give you their ideas, and may not ask you for assistance.

The problem of fear usually appears when people are faced with new situations or doing new things. It is reasonable for people to be concerned about their performance, whether they will be able to do something new successfully. This concern usually leads people to take extra precautions and perform more carefully so success does occur. When people believe (anticipate) they will not be able to perform successfully and they think the consequence of failure is important to them, they will perform badly or not at all.

Picture the bank teller who is so concerned about making errors in handling cash, he counts money in slow motion and creates customer lines out to the street. Or the salesperson who is so afraid of the customer saying no, he or she does not ask the customer to buy the product and therefore never achieves sales targets. And how about the newly promoted supervisor who avoids correcting employee performance problems because he or she fears social rejection from these former fellow workers? You might say, "But don't they realize they could lose their jobs and that is more important than a few errors or social rejection?" The answer is, "No, not at the time; they are concentrating on the wrong consequences."

This problem is not related to situations in which there are real and serious negative consequences to employees for performing, such as rushing into burning buildings or raging rivers to save people. It is related to situations in which most employees do the job or task but one or more employees are afraid to; they anticipate a negative consequence to themselves for doing it.

PREVENTIVE SOLUTION

1. If there are no negative consequences for the things you want your employees to do, explain that to them early in their employment. One of the purposes of giving orientation to new employees is to explain the relationships—how the game is played in your organization. Let them know:

   a. It is okay to argue with the boss.
   b. No question is a dumb question.
   c. You prefer that employees ask you to repeat instructions several times rather than do something wrong.
   d. Employees should try to be innovative to improve the way things are done as long as new ideas are cleared with you ahead of time.
   e. You don't punish employees for failure when they are trying to help you.

   In other words, you want all your employees

to know there are no negative consequences to them for trying to do what they are supposed to do.

2. The next step is to prove that anticipated negative consequences are actually not there by controlling how you respond when employees do the things you want them to do. How you respond day to day will eventually convince them that what you say is true. Become conscious of your facial expressions so you can avoid broadcasting your annoyances and frustrations to your people.

3. It is your job to convince employees that some anticipated negative consequences are not as painful as they expect them to be. There are situations in life where negative consequences for appropriate performance cannot be avoided, but it helps to put them in perspective. For example, trying to do a swan dive off the diving board the first few times may result in some hard, flat, painful contact with the water. It hurts when you do it, but it doesn't disable you for life.

4. When discussing ideas with people it is certainly possible that when you disagree with someone's ideas, he or she will argue. But an argument, although unpleasant, is not the end of the relationship. And when a person asks questions or presents ideas, occasionally the response of others is to laugh or be sarcastic. Although that may be unpleasant at that time, it should not be viewed as some lasting punishing event.

12

There Is No Negative Consequence to Them for Poor Performance

DO YOU HAVE AN EMPLOYEE WHO DOES NOT FOLLOW PROCE-dure or work rules and has been doing that for a year or more? Did you inherit an employee in your department described by her previous manager as being uncooperative and disruptive since she was hired several years ago? Do you have an employee whom you don't ask anymore to submit a report because he refuses to write reports? Do you have an employee in your company who never does certain parts of his job because he doesn't like those tasks? When you initiate disciplinary action with an employee who refuses to perform, do you get pressure from higher management, the personnel department, or the union representative that you are being hard-nosed and you are forced to back off? If your answer is "yes" to these questions, you have employees who are not performing because "There is no negative consequence to them for poor performance."

THE PROBLEM

Unfortunately, what many managers view as a punishment to an employee may not be a punishment to the employee. Have you ever seen an employee's personnel folder bulging with reprimands and low performance appraisal ratings and the employee is still on the job performing badly? The manager passed out what appeared to be punishment, but it did not seem to have any effect.

Close examination may even reveal that bad performers receive raises and choice work assignments according to seniority in spite of their bad performance.

If most managers were told that the boss was going to put a reprimand in their folders, the reaction would be highly emotional because managers view reprimands as punishment. We assume lower-level employees would respond the same way. If, however, you examine the use of reprimands in business, you frequently find that putting a reprimand in an employee's folder results in nothing more than that—another piece of paper in the folder.

Written and verbal reprimands are only a part of what is referred to as progressive discipline. The assumption is that the discipline progresses in severity from warnings to reprimands to time off without pay as the performance discrepancy continues. In many companies the paperwork piles up in the employee's folder but the severity of the discipline does not increase. Also, for some people, being told to go home for three days without pay is not punishment.

Many times I have heard workers comment about poor performers, "Why doesn't the company get rid of that 'goof-off'?" I have heard union representatives say, "I wish the company would get smart and fire that 'screwup' and eliminate all these hassles." Yet no one gets fired. I know of one employee who was fired because he hit his boss with a tire iron in the company parking lot but was hired back nine months later as part of union contract negotiation. In one company a laboratory technician who had been reprimanded several times for not wearing safety glasses, among other things, finally arrived in the laboratory one day wearing the glasses. When his supervisor complimented him on wearing the safety glasses, the technician reached up and wiggled his fingers through the empty glass frames. He had actually taken the time to remove the glass from the frame so he could play his game with his supervisor. He was still on the payroll one year later.

I ask managers, "If an employee performing an important task does it wrong on purpose and no matter how hard you try to correct the situation, the employee doesn't improve, would you fire him?" Frequently, the surprising answer is, "No." When I ask, "Would you demote that person?" the frequent answer is, "No, we don't do that around here." I ask them, "Would you deny that person a raise?" The startling response they give at times is, "Well, except for a minimum raise to cover the cost of living, we would not give that person a raise." In other words, bad performers get raises.

Another amazingly common practice in some large, apparently well-organized companies is that managers faced with a poor performer suggest that the employee request a transfer to some other unit. As a result, there are poor performers working in that company for as long as 18 years who have never worked for any boss who thought their performance was appropriate, but the employees remain on the payroll.

A lot of managers tell me that they give above-average performance appraisal ratings to below-average performers because they don't want to be the one to put a black mark on an employee's record forever. Some managers have told me they give big raises to bad performers in the hope it will motivate them to perform better.

When you are trying to understand why your employees don't do what they are supposed to do and none of the reasons mentioned previously are the reasons for nonperformance, the reason may be, "There is no negative consequence to them for performing badly."

PREVENTIVE SOLUTION

1. You must intervene in your organization so there are negative consequences to employees whose persistent bad performance is willful misconduct; they are choosing to perform inappropriately.

2. In some work situations, there is no negative consequence for poor performance because management does not know the subordinate is failing. Either the subordinate's performance is not checked by the boss or when the checking is done, the mistakes cannot be traced to

an individual performer. For example, in work situations where employees are assigned a different vehicle or piece of equipment each workday, the vehicles or equipment are usually in deplorable condition as a result of employee abuse. The abuse cannot be pinpointed; any employee can say, "I didn't do it; it was that way when I got it." But when employees are permanently assigned to drive the same vehicle or operate the same equipment every day, there is less abuse. Because permanent assignments make abuse traceable, there is a negative consequence for employees abusing their equipment.

The practice of requiring inspectors, or packers, or assemblers to put their names on a slip of paper that accompanies the product to the ultimate user has increased over the last 30 years. Instituting such a practice usually improves the quality of the items or process or service involved. The explanation for the improvement usually alludes to some high-sounding concepts, such as pride of performance. But on a more basic level, putting your name on what you service, assemble, or inspect means that if you do it wrong, it will eventually be traced back to you. There will be a negative consequence for bad performance.

3. When employees doing work they like to do perform badly (willfully), assign work they do not like to do.

4. When an employee having a desirable work location willfully performs badly, assign a less desirable work location.

5. When an employee who is normally permitted to attend outside activities during work hours or at company expense willfully performs the job badly, deny those privileges.

6. When an employee willfully performs badly, demote him or her.

7. When an employee willfully performs badly, deny or delay raises until performance improves.

8. When an employee is demoted because of poor performance, reduce the salary.

9. When an employee who has expressed an interest in promotion willfully performs badly, explain in writing that this willful nonperformance is considered unreliability, and therefore future promotion will not be considered unless performance improves.

10. Change your rules about transfers. An employee willfully performing badly in a current job should not be eligible for transfer unless the willful misconduct is corrected for a minimum of six months. Anyone performing badly for other reasons should not be transferred unless the task performed badly is not a part of the new job.

11. When it seems clear that a person is willfully not improving performance, and your coaching discussions fail, terminate the employment.[3]

12. When these solutions change performance, be sure to give a positive consequence to maintain the improvement.

13. Have you ever had the feeling that your employees' performance improves somewhat

when you appear in their work space? If so, you have discovered one of the most powerful management interventions to increase productivity. One negative consequence to poor performance is your appearance in their work space. Increase your frequency of appearing in their work space as follow up and you will get more increases in productivity. The reason for this effect is that you, the boss, are a moving negative consequence, the catcher of poor performance. You are not a bad person; you are merely the last person they want to see if they are goofing off.

So increase your frequency of appearing in the work space of the nonperformers and ask questions such as, "How are you doing?" "What are you doing?" "Why are you doing that?" "When will you begin (doing the right thing)?" "When will you end what you are working on?"

The more frequently you appear in your employees' work environment, the more you will have the happy experience of catching people doing things right. You will increase your opportunities to reinforce performance with verbal rewards. You will also catch more poor performance sooner so that you can help prevent big problems. Initially you will get resistance from some employees accusing you of checking up on them. Your response should be, "You are right. That's what I get paid to do."

I am not suggesting a total management approach of talking loudly, carrying a big stick, and dreaming up ways of threatening and punishing the people who work for you. That is what ineffective managers do.

What I am telling you is that there are real work situations where none of the other reasons for nonperformance discussed so far are the reasons for nonperformance. The only reason this employee is misperforming willfully is because there is no negative consequence to him or her for doing it that way. If you don't take appropriate action to correct the problem, you will have to live with it. You owe it to all the employees who do things right to take action against the employees who choose to do things wrong.

13

Obstacles Beyond Their Control

"OBSTACLES BEYOND EMPLOYEES' CONTROL" MEANS REAL barriers preventing an employee from performing. For example, if I was showing a video during a seminar and the building electrical power failed, and there was no backup generator, I could still talk to the participants, but I could not show the video. If seeing the video was critically important to the seminar, there would be nothing I could do to overcome that obstacle at that time. Sometimes an obstacle bars performance only because the employee doesn't know how to get around the obstacle. In that situation, the obstacle is not an obstacle to everyone, it is just an obstacle to that employee. Unfortunately, when employees tell the boss about an obstacle hurting their performance, the boss's common response is to accuse the employees of merely giving excuses or having a poor attitude.

THE PROBLEM

One company that produced a software product to handle record keeping and billing processes in doctors' offices decided to sell the same system to other kinds of businesses. When the sales managers advised the president that the product was not selling because the system could not do the more complicated job required by other businesses, the president's response was, "You just don't know how to sell." The salespeople were initially able to sell a product that did not work until enough customers spread the word about the product. The president of that company was ignoring the facts and doing his emperor thing: "The world is as I say it is."

A manager in another company recently described a problem he was having with one of his field engineers who was abrupt and unresponsive to customers and was generating a lot of customer complaints. Every time the manager discussed the problem with the engineer, the engineer went around the manager to complain to the company president (a friend). As a result, the engineer's manager was told by the president to leave the engineer alone. In this situation, there is an obstacle beyond the control of the engineer's manager. Because the manager cannot take any disciplinary action, the engineer is now unmanageable.

This reason for nonperformance includes all those situations, conditions, and influences outside the individual that are preventing performance from occurring. Following are some examples.

Resources not available. There are very few jobs or tasks performed in an organization that are begun and completed totally by a single individual, whether in manufacturing, accounting, or health care. Work is usually a sequence of tasks performed by two or more individuals. If the first employee's performance is late or incomplete, the next employee is faced with an obstacle.

- In a crowded restaurant, if the busboys are not cleaning the tables quickly enough, the maitre d' cannot seat people from the long line of waiting customers.

- In that same environment, a waiter cannot deliver the meal if the cook has not finished cooking it.

- In a hospital environment, something as simple as shaving a patient's skin area targeted for a surgical operation is one of the prerequisites before delivering the patient to the operating room. If the patient is not shaved, the operation cannot begin.

- A surgeon cannot begin the surgical operation until the anesthesiologist anesthetizes the patient.

- In a clerical environment, if someone has not collected the required data, the next person to deal with that data is unable to enter it in the computer or analyze it.

- In a production situation, an employee is unable to drill holes if there are no parts available to be drilled, or an employee cannot complete assembly of a device if just one screw is unavailable.

- One of your recent commercial flights might have been delayed because the ground crew was late refueling the aircraft.

○ In the summertime in New York City, occasionally firemen have insufficient water pressure in their hoses to fight fires because the children in the surrounding neighborhoods have illegally opened fire hydrants to create cooling showers.

Poor quality of resources.   Resources delivered on time but unusable become an obstacle. The following are examples:

○ Data received with errors

○ The spring collection of blouses delivered to the department store in the wrong distribution of sizes

○ Raw materials that do not meet the required specifications, such as contaminated chemicals, dyes of the wrong color, structural nails and rivets of the wrong length or diameter, building materials of insufficient strength or flexibility, fluctuations in electrical power

Conflicting instructions.   Unbelievable as it may seem, there are work situations where employees receive instructions from their boss and their boss's boss about the same job or task, and the instructions are in conflict. This situation is usually rampant in family-owned organizations where the founder as well as the children work for the organization. The founder of the company, who may be president or chairman of the board, ignores several levels of managers, giving instructions directly to the lowest-level employee. The instructions may be good for the moment but frequently are in discontinuity with the total situation and in conflict with what the employee's direct supervisor has instructed. Confusion and wasted resources are the only outcome of this kind of mismanagement.

Other examples of obstacles beyond the employees' control would be authority not delegated with the work assignment, equipment malfunctioning, service departments refusing to provide service, strikes, floods, earthquakes, holidays, snowbound roads, siesta time, war, and so on.

Obstacles can be classified into three categories. CATEGORY ONE are those situations where conditions exist outside the employee that prevent the employee (or any employee) from performing the task appropriately in any way.

CATEGORY TWO are those situations where a condition exists outside the employee that prevents this employee from performing the task appropriately the way he or she always does it, only because he or she does not know how to overcome it. In other words, there is something or someone actively or passively preventing this employee from performing only because this employee does not know the possible ways of getting around the obstacle. For example, your employee does not complete a report on time because someone else did not deliver needed information. You ask that employee, "Why didn't you go over there and get the information rather than waiting for them to deliver it?" Your employee replies, "I didn't know I was permitted to do that." Your employee was not aware of that alternative to get around the obstacle.

CATEGORY THREE are those situations where conditions exist outside the employee that prevent this employee from performing the task appropriately because he lacks the skill to use available alternatives. In other words, the employee is aware of something that could be done to get around the obstacle but does not know how to do it. For example, if I am on a camping trip and must start a fire but have no matches or other fire-starting instruments, I am faced with an obstacle. However, I know that a fire could be started by rubbing two sticks together in a certain way, but I don't know how to do that. As another example, my secretary was supposed to give me a computer printout of a special report I need for a breakfast meeting tomorrow, but he left for vacation without doing it. I know the computer will print it for me, but I don't know the codes and how to operate his computer so it will print the report.

PREVENTIVE SOLUTION

1. Remove the obstacle and performance will come back to normal. When your employees advise you that they are unable to perform because of an obstacle beyond their control, don't tell them to work it out themselves. Get involved in the situation; investigate it. Don't relegate your employees' complaints about non-cooperation from other departments, poor materials, or malfunctioning equipment as bad attitude or lack of creativity. It is your job to remove the obstacles that are preventing your employees from performing. Don't be like one manager I knew who put a sign over his office door which read, "If you don't have a solution,

don't bring me your problem." As you might guess, there were lots of problems in his unit not getting solved.

2. When your employees are unable to perform because of inappropriate performance by other units in your organization, collect the facts. It may be necessary to get the managers of those other units involved to eliminate the problem. Sometimes this may require changing procedures and methods.

   If you can't get your suppliers to deliver the right materials on time, change suppliers.

   If you have multiple levels of management giving the same employees conflicting instructions, stop doing that. If it is your boss doing that, explain the problem and beg your boss to work through you. If you can't get your boss to stop going around you, giving conflicting instructions to your employees, work out a plan with the employees on what to do when that occurs. Otherwise, that obstacle will cause performance problems and cost your organization net dollars and perhaps cost you your job.

   When an employee is unsuccessful in negotiating at their level to obtain improved service from other units, intervene in those negotiations to help achieve that change. By doing that you remove the obstacle.

3. If you can't remove an obstacle, give employees a strategy for overcoming it and/or teach them the skill to use that strategy. For example, if your salespeople cannot get the sale because of price objections, teach them how to overcome price objections.

4. It is not effective problem solving or effective management to buck the problem back to the subordinate. It is also not effective to wait for the obstacle to cause performance problems before you teach employees how to deal with common obstacles. The best *preventive management* approach is to prepare your employees in advance. Forecast the obstacles they may face in the future and give them the strategies and skills in advance to overcome those obstacles. If you initiate the corrective solution, you will help your employees avoid nonperformance. For example, if you tell your employees in advance that they should go to other departments to get information when it is not delivered, they will discover two things: there is an alternative for overcoming that obstacle, and that is part of their job.

5. If you can't remove an obstacle or give a strategy for overcoming the obstacle, you had better give employees something else to do because they are not going to do what they are supposed to do.[4] The employee is now failing because "No one could do it."

14

Their
Personal Limits
Prevent Them
from Performing

NONPERFORMANCE "BECAUSE OF PERSONAL LIMITS" IS A POP-
ular choice with managers when they are trying to
escape blame or are not responsible for correcting
performance problems. This reason is commonly
used when describing employees not working for
that manager, such as people two or more levels
below or even in other departments. The typical
expressions are, "It's just a wrong hire," or "You can't
put a square peg in a round hole, you know," or "He
is not a self-starter." Maybe you have heard the one
"She has sawdust for brains." In some eastern coun-
tries a common phrase is "He missed the bus" or "He
missed the boat." The one I like best is "When God
was handing out brains, she (employee) was on a coffee break." There are many more descriptions managers use, some more colorful and some unprintable.
But all are expressing the same thing: the manager
believes the employee is failing because of some
inherent personal limit in the employee.

THE PROBLEM

There certainly are situations when employees fail because of personal limits, but these situations rarely occur as frequently as managers claim. "Personal limits" means individual physical limits that are unchangeable and that are, in fact, preventing job performance. For example, if the job requires someone who is not color-blind and the employee is color-blind, that would be a personal limit. If the job requires highly accurate depth perception and this employee only has one eye, you will not have highly accurate depth perception. If the job requires ten fingers to perform it and this employee has only nine, and it cannot be done with nine fingers, that would be a personal limit. If you assume that IQ measures intelligence and this job requires an IQ of 125, and the employee has an IQ of 65, that would be a personal limit.

A personal limit is not a deficiency that is a function of learning. For example, if you hired me as your corporate pilot but I didn't know how to fly, I would not be failing as a pilot because of a personal limit, I would be failing because I didn't know how to fly. If you taught me how to fly, the reason for my nonperformance would disappear. My "not knowing" how to fly without training is totally different from my "not being able" to fly no matter how much training you give me. Unfortunately, flying as a skill is more obvious to observe than the many less measurable skills you assume your employees possess.

One of managers' biggest errors is to treat situations of "not knowing" as situations of "personal limit," so they do not attempt to solve the problem. From my observations in business, at least 80 percent of the people who are identified as failing because of *personal limits* are not actually failing for that reason. They are failing because they were never taught how to do it. A good case in point is giving speeches to groups. It is common to label an employee who does this badly as missing some vital and irreplaceable quality, when in actuality giving a speech is a skill. This is proved every day by the seeming transformation of poor speech makers who graduate from Dale Carnegie. I know one employee who would literally regurgitate her breakfast when faced with making a sales call. But after completing a 15-week public speaking course with Dale Carnegie, she was able to approach her selling job effectively. If you observed this employee before she completed the course, you would have concluded, "She just doesn't have it." But the "it" she didn't have was the "knowing how."

Personal limits can be divided into two categories: *permanent* and *temporary*. Color blindness is an example of a permanent limit only for jobs requiring proper color discrimination. In jobs requiring stereoscopic vision, such as brain surgery, having one eye would hinder performance. Short stature has been a problem where normal height is needed and a platform could not be used. In some jobs, certain physical dexterity is needed to perform appropriately. A bank teller, for example, must have at least average finger dexterity to handle and count cash quickly enough to provide fast customer service. A teller with average dexterity and a teller with below-average dexterity will both improve with practice, but the below-average-dexterity teller will not become quick enough. In certain customer service work, a severely abnormal facial appearance could be a problem if customers are repulsed and avoid that person when seeking service. The employee may perform the job function perfectly, but if customers avoid that person, there is a problem. But note that the term "repulsed" could be somewhat easier to define than "not attractive enough." Several saleswomen have described their problem to me as being too attractive. They said they had to dress down to move the customer's concentration from themselves to the products they were trying to sell. There could be a lot of disagreement among people trying to define what is "attractive"; just take a look at who your neighbor married.

Limited intelligence is usually viewed as a problem by managers, but the term "intelligence" is too broad to classify. Does intelligence mean analytical ability, idea fluency, memory, verbal acuity, attention span, awareness, or visualization? Real mental incapacities are not hard to miss, but a close look at the so-called intelligence problems can usually be traced to "not knowing" and "not enough practice."

A temporary personal limit is one which could be corrected or perhaps would eventually go away all by itself. Pregnancy could be a temporary limit depending upon what work was required and how far along the pregnancy had progressed. The limit of not being able to speak a foreign language could be eliminated with lessons or even a phrase book. Blocked nasal passages and laryngitis don't last forever. Alcoholism and drug addiction and mental illness would be considered a temporary personal limit. A manager who goes into a 30-second rage three times a day and admits he can't control himself is merely mentally ill for 30 seconds three times a day. Problems described as unfriendliness, or insensitivity, or abrasiveness would be problems of behavior, not necessarily mental illness. Those people may simply need acting lessons and some of the other preventive actions, such as feedback, knowing what to do, training in how to do it, and verbal recognition for improvements. Sometimes people are ill and don't know it. Many so-called mental problems, such as disruptive, destructive, or antisocial behavior and even paranoia, can be traced to chemical imbalances in the brain such as occur with hypoglycemia (low blood sugar). The weird behavior usually disappears within several months following proper changes in the person's diet. Perhaps some of those weird people working for you are not born wrong; they only need to change their diet, but they don't know it.

Usually when we get this far in our discussion in seminars, managers say, "These kinds of things are not what I am talking about when I talk about personal limits." And my response is, "If you are not talking about these kinds of things, you are not talking about personal limits, you are talking about some other reason for nonperformance." "You are right," they say. "I guess I was lumping a lot of different things under personal limits." Personal limits is not a frequent reason for employee failure; it is just mentioned frequently by managers.

PREVENTIVE SOLUTION

1. Accept the fact that when you are talking about personal limits, you are talking about an individ-

ual's capacity. "Capacity" is defined in psychology as the highest level of performance the individual can achieve, with maximum assistance. The limits of capacity would be genetic or damage caused by an accident or illness. Capacity is different from "ability," which is a function of learning. Also notice the reference to "maximum assistance" in defining capacity. If someone is failing to do something but that person has not received maximum assistance, you could not say the reason for failure was a lack of capacity or a personal limit.

2. Accept the fact that you only need normal people to do your work at any level, not Olympic athletes. You don't need the best of the best of the best to perform your daily work. You couldn't afford to pay for that quality of person, and there are not that many available.

3. If there are critical personal limits that relate to success or failure in a particular job, be sure to evaluate the applicant before hiring or promotion to determine whether those personal limits exist. Consider using appropriate testing to give you objective information to help your judgment.

4. When talking about performance problems, describe the specific problem, the things done wrong or not done right. Don't use metaphors such as "a bad apple" or "out in left field"; they are too general and will lead you to wrong conclusions about the reasons for nonperformance and subsequently to the wrong preventive solution.

5. Don't be too quick to label your nonperformer as failing because of personal limits. It will usually be the last reason for nonperformance.

Before you decide to replace an employee, ask yourself:

—"Is this one of those rare situations where I, the manager, made that possible, but improbable, mistake of failing to teach this employee how to do what it is we want done?"

It costs you nothing to ask that question; it will cost you quite a lot if you get the wrong answer; employee turnover is expensive. Review the employee's performance relative to all the other possible reasons why employees don't do what they are supposed to do.

6. Collect some information such as the following before you make your decision:

   a. Ask the employee, "Could you please tell me how you are supposed to do that task?"
   b. If he gives you the right answer, ask him to do it while you observe to see if he follows all the correct steps.
   c. If he doesn't give you the right answer or doesn't do it correctly, walk him through a detailed demonstration of what he is supposed to do and then repeat "b."

7. If a permanent personal limit really is causing failure, there is nothing you can do about it other than replace the person or live with the problem.

15

Personal Problems

Now we come to the big one: the reason for nonperformance common in all work situations and one of the biggest frustrations for managers. Most managers don't even know how to talk about personal problems, much less deal with them. Without solutions and with no training at all, managers vacillate between their responsibilities to the organization and their concern to be an understanding, sensitive, and helpful human being. Managers vary from the extremes of playing marriage counselor, confessor, parent, psychologist, and money lender to being judge and executioner. The process consumes a lot of time and sometimes nothing works.

THE PROBLEM

"Personal problems" refers to those happenings in a person's private life outside the work environment that appear to be reasons for nonperformance on the job. These problems could be family arguments, divorce, unreliable baby-sitters, sick children, car troubles, unreliable car pools, death in the family, unsatisfied gambling debts, trouble with in-laws, etc., etc., etc. Personal illness would not be included in this category because it is considered a "temporary personal limit," not a personal problem. Of course, employees could become mentally ill because of their personal problems, but that would move them into the other category of personal limits.

Usually employee personal problems are not difficult to detect if they affect performance. For example:

○ Employees who spend excessive time on the phone handling personal problems

○ Employees who are working less or are producing errors because they spend a lot of time talking to fellow employees about their personal problems

○ Employees who abuse your equipment or slam down phones or are abrupt with customers because they are having problems at home

○ Employees who arrive for work late and leave early because of unreliable baby-sitters

When you ask employees why their performance is slow, inaccurate, or weird, they reply:

○ "I have things on my mind."

○ "I just can't keep my mind on my work."

○ "I am having personal problems and I would rather not discuss it."

Most companies provide employees time off from work to take care of personal problems. Almost all organizations have a funeral leave policy providing an allowable number of paid days off when there is a death in the immediate family. Some companies provide a set number of personal days per year that can be used for dental appointments, picking up an uncle at the airport, or visiting a child's teacher. Except for death in the family, it is usually required that time off be scheduled in advance so management is able to plan around the absence.

Recent studies have shown that personal problems which cause tension, frustration, and anger frequently affect how employees deal with customers, fellow workers, and even the boss. But there is no direct connection between any particular personal problem and any particular response. There are some people who experience things which you and I would consider quite horrible, yet you would never know it from their calm outward appearance. And there are people who "blow up" or "fall apart" when experiencing what we might consider an insignificant personal problem. A foreman in a large automotive plant told me that he was frustrated by an employee who would fly into a rage and call for his union representative every time the foreman said "good morning" to him. The foreman had no explanation for this weird behavior. Two years later I met that employee in one of my seminars and he voluntarily described his reaction. When I asked him why he reacted with such rage when his foreman said "good morning," he said, "I was having a lot of problems with divorce, finances, and the children, and I didn't want that foreman telling me I was having a good morning." I explained to him that the greeting "good morning" was actually a shortened version of "I wish you a good morning," which meant the foreman was not stating the current status of his morning but hoping he would have a good one. He said, "I didn't realize that."

But there are performance problems on the job that appear to be caused by personal problems not covered by company policies and that occur only because the boss permits them to occur. Frequently managers permit an employee to not perform because that employee has a personal problem, yet the manager had that same problem in the past and performed in spite of it. In other words, the personal problem was not the reason for nonperformance; it was the boss's permission for it to be a reason for nonperformance.

One salesman explained to me that because of his divorce the previous year he had been unable to work. Both he and his boss knew he didn't go to work, not even for one day, for three months. He said, "I didn't go to work because I was depressed; therefore, isn't divorce a reason for nonperformance?" My response was to tell him that part of the therapy for depression is activity and work. His boss was, in fact, supporting his depression rather than helping eliminate it. "But I was really upset," he said. I asked him what he would do if he owned a restaurant and one of his three waiters announced that he was going through a divorce, was depressed, and therefore would not come to work for the next three months and expected to be paid for the time off. He said he wouldn't pay the waiter. When I asked him why not, he said, "I don't think I could afford to pay three months' pay for no work."

If we could roll back the clock and tell the salesman's manager that the salesman's three months' pay for no work would come out of the manager's pocket, do you think the salesman would have been permitted the time off? Of course, the answer is no and this leads to one of the reasons why personal problems are handled badly from the organization's point of view. Managers are not giving away their own money, they are giving away someone else's money: the corporate net dollars. It is easy for managers to be magnanimous with someone else's money and permit nonperformance because of personal problems. Accepting responsibility (or being held responsible) for the money can change a manager's response from: "I understand how you feel; why don't you stay home today," to "I understand how you feel and I wish I could give you the day off, but it is not my money, and we need you today." The first response is sensitive and irresponsible; the second response is sensitive and responsible and describes reality.

There are situations where the time off or nonperformance is justified, as with an accident or an illness to a loved one, or for important legal matters. However, there is a big difference between feeling bad about losing your bowling ball and losing your child. Even in companies where 2 to 4 days of excused absence is allowed as funeral leave, it is not allowed for any deceased relative. It is usually specified that the relative must be spouse, mother, father, or blood relative who resides as a permanent member of the household. The neighbor, old college roommate, or favorite dog doesn't count for funeral leave. Funeral leave is a good example of the company deciding and formalizing how much compassion managers are permitted vis-à-vis a personal problem. The company does not know if you will be shedding tears for those 2 to 4 days or sighing "good riddance" over a cool beer; they have merely organized the manager's response to that personal problem.

This brings us to the second reason why personal problems are handled badly and at times unfairly. Since most of the common personal problem situations are not addressed by the company with specified guidelines as with funeral leave, each manager is left to decide independently about each personal problem, like an emperor or empress dispensing largess. Inevitably, the desire to be viewed as understanding, sensitive, and helpful by employees wins out. Managers don't know which personal problems should be permitted to be reasons for nonperformance or when it is okay for the employee to feel bad but not okay for the employee to work bad.

The third reason managers have so much difficulty dealing with personal problems is that they don't know how to talk about personal problems or how involved they should get. Hence, there is a lot of amateur counseling going on. Therefore, one of the reasons some employees seem to occupy an inordinate amount of the manager's time with personal problems is because that is the only time the employee gets "nice" attention from the manager. Chapter 7 discussed how behavior followed by a positive consequence will increase in its frequency. That rule about human behavior works whether or not the behavior is desirable. If the only time an employee receives understanding, sensitive, helpful attention from the boss is when talking about personal problems, you can bet that personal problem discussions will increase in frequency.

Another thing to consider is that it is common for all normal human beings while working to have thoughts about things other than work. These thoughts can cover the spectrum from birth to death and everything in between but not necessarily be about problems. When employees perform badly because they have something on their mind, it does not have to be thoughts about accident or illness; it could be thoughts about what a wonderful night they had last night or anticipation of how wonderful tonight will be. These non-work-related thoughts are only a problem when they become a distraction to appropriate work performance. Most managers would have no difficulty saying, "Could you please get your mind off your happy love life and concentrate on the problem we are trying to solve." But they wouldn't dare say, "Could you please get your mind off your broken marriage and concentrate on the problem we are trying to solve." Yet the reason for the performance problem is the same: the employee is thinking about something else. Managers believe they have the right to interfere with pleasant "daydreaming" but not with unpleasant "daydreaming" (worries).

PREVENTIVE SOLUTION

1. Recognize that home life is becoming more important to people and the increase in single-parent homes is changing people's priorities relative to long work hours, business travel, and relocation. But realize that at least half of the personal problems that appear to be reasons for

work nonperformance are reasons for nonperformance only because managers permit them to be reasons.

2. Employee personal problems you face at work can be divided into two categories: the emotional category and the time-off category. The emotional category covers everything from blank stares and listlessness, up through complaining to anyone who will listen, to emotional breakdowns with tears (yelling perhaps) and excessive time in the rest room recovering. The time-off category can be further divided into two categories: the *emergency-related* such as emergency family illness, child day care failures (nonrecurring), automobile problems (nonrecurring), accidents, and *personal business,* such as renewing a driver's license, closing on a new house, legal and dental appointments, and so on.

3. Permit employees to take time off to handle personal business, such as visiting teachers at school and seeing lawyers or orthodontists. It is okay to permit employees to start work late some days and leave work early on other days to handle personal business. You can ask employees to make up lost time in the future when it is more convenient for them as well as the organization. But the personal business time off should always be planned with advanced notice, preferably conducted during nonworking hours or non-peak-workload hours and, depending on the time and frequency needed, could be charged to the employee's vacation time. Some companies lump all allowable time off for vacation, sick leave, etc., into one total called personal days. An employee can use

these days any way he chooses. It eliminates a lot of unnecessary discussion about time off.

4. The emergency-related time off, although a nuisance to organized business activities, is most critically important to the employee and must be responded to by managers as a first priority. Organize assistance, provide for work coverage, do it yourself if necessary, but expedite the employee's response to the emergency.

5. How you manage the emotional category depends on how much of a problem it is. Some of your employees will have serious personal problems and no one at work, including you, will know about it. Other employees will have minor personal problems and everyone will know about it whether they want to or not. Make yourself available to employees who want to talk to you about their personal problems. Merely talking about a problem frequently helps people find their own solution or helps them live with the problem. If they are emotionally upset but performing appropriately, you don't have a performance problem; you are merely helping to brighten their lives. But don't play amateur psychologist or marriage counselor because you will fail. Help them find the needed professional counseling or assistance.

6. For those situations where there is a personal problem but performance must occur, do the following:

   a. Discuss the problem in detail and try to help the employee's personal problems go away by directing the person to sources of assistance.

b. If the employee's problem cannot be eliminated, explain that there really are two problems. The employee's personal problem is one problem, and the employee's not performing the work is a second problem.

c. Explain that it is understandable that personal problems may not go away quickly, but the work problem must go away quickly. For example, it would be okay to say, "I am sorry that your marriage is breaking up and I can see how this emotional situation may last a year. Unfortunately, my work problems cannot continue for a year. Since I can't make your problem go away, can you help make my work problem go away?"

d. Ask for the employee's cooperation in eliminating the work problem. You will be amazed at the positive responses you will get.

7. Identify which personal problems your organization will accept as reasons for nonperformance on the job so all of your managers are following the same guidelines. Make provisions for people to handle or respond to those personal problems in planned ways. Create a handbook to guide your managers in dealing with personal problems and include names and phone numbers of professionals to whom you can refer employees who need help.

8. Realize that you, as a manager, do not have the arbitrary right to excuse people from working for any reasons you or they choose. Teamwork means following the team rules.

9. If you examine how man performs in life in general, you will discover that most people outside

the work environment do things in their social life that they must do in spite of personal problems. I am not suggesting that you tell your employees they should not be bothered by personal problems. I am suggesting that you tell them it is okay to be bothered by personal problems as long as they do what they are supposed to on the job. This is not a wild or heartless idea; this is a therapeutic concept that helps people achieve.

16

No One Could Do It

When I ask managers, "Why don't your employees do what they are supposed to do?" one answer given is, "They don't have enough time." When I ask, "Do you mean you give them more work than can be done in the available time?" they answer, "Yes." In other words, managers ask employees to do three one-hour tasks in two hours and no one could do that.

THE PROBLEM

This reason should not be confused with the creative or innovative approach attempting to get employees to do things that no one has previously been able to do. If that were your goal, you would not merely be assigning tasks or projects, you would be using brainstorming, work planning, and other creativity management techniques to help your employees develop strategies for doing the seemingly impossible. It is perfectly appropriate to discuss a task that no one has been able to do so far and to search for possible ways to do that task.

This problem does not refer to asking someone to do three one-hour jobs in two hours, which you could do but they can't do. Obviously, if you could do it, it can be done. The problem in this example is that the employees don't know how to do what you know how to do in two hours. This is a training problem. If you give these employees training and practice in doing it your way, they could also do it.

PREVENTIVE SOLUTION

1. "No one could do it" is one of the few reasons for nonperformance rarely given by managers. In my own personal experience as a manager and consultant, I have rarely come across this reason for nonperformance. But as a professional manager, you should be aware that it could occur.

2. If workers could in fact not do it, give them something else to do. There are no other alternatives available to you.

3. Use your resources in ways that permit people to perform.

Part II

Preventive Management: A New Management System That Gets You the Best Results

17

How to Use the Power of Preventive Management to Get Perfect Performance

IF, AT THIS POINT, I ASKED YOU WHY EMPLOYEES DON'T DO what they are supposed to do, you would probably answer, "Poor management." Except for failure because of *personal problems* or because of *personal limits,* or *no one could do it,* and perhaps a few *obstacles,* everything else we discussed could be subcategories under the heading of poor management. Even failure related to personal problems could be decreased if managers would realize that all personal problems may be reasons for feeling bad but are not necessarily reasons for working badly. Managers are also not blameless for failure related to personal limits because a manager hired or promoted the employees in the first place. And analysis shows that 80 percent of the people blamed for having personal limits are actually failing because of some of the reasons already discussed.

You should also conclude that a large part of the manager's job is to deliver consequences to employees for performance where no consequence or the wrong consequences are occurring. In a seminar a manager asked, "Why is it that employees playing company softball after work put out ten times more energy than when they are doing their job?" "The reason," I told him, "is consequences and feedback." In a softball game and in most sports there are feedback and positive and negative consequences following performance every few minutes. At work it is difficult to find work-related negative or positive consequence to employees or feedback in the entire day. If you want people to act on the job the way they act in sports, create more frequent feedback and more frequent positive consequences for good work.

So if these reasons why people at work don't do what they are supposed to do are caused by poor management, the obvious solution is to apply good management as interventions to make these reasons go away or to prevent them from occurring. If this is so obvious, you might wonder why managers don't take actions to prevent each of these reasons for nonperformance from occurring. As one answer, we discovered that managers were unaware of these specific causes of nonperformance because they thought about people performance problems in general terms and described them with metaphors like "not cutting the mustard." A second reason was that the manager's analysis was limited to the same one or two reasons, such as, "They are not motivated" or "They are unqualified for the job." "Motivation" is the most misunderstood and most overused word in business in discussing people's performance.

We also discovered that managers had some erroneous beliefs about human behavior that were to them a logical reason for not taking corrective action. For example, when we taught managers that their verbal compliments about an employee's good performance were a powerful influence on job performance, many managers said, "I pay them for that. Why should I thank them for it?" The answer, of course, is, "To get what you pay for." A lot of managers believe they should not have to work at getting people to do what they are paid to do.

This belief is based on the predominant unwritten and unproven theory that if you hire the right welder, or the right Ph.D. chemist, or the right senior accountant, the job will get done without the boss's help. In other words, if you put the *right* people on the job, you will not have to manage them. If this theory were true, a lot of managers could be eliminated; all your organization would need is a lot of good recruiters. It is really amazing that so many intelligent people believe such a ridiculous idea. That approach is not management; it is hoping for the best.

In the past we managed our business machines and equipment that way only to discover it was a dumb idea. In the early years of manufacturing, managers bought the best production machines and ran them until they stopped running. Eventually it was discovered that machine "downtime" was nonproduction time; when machines were not running, employees were not producing products, although overhead continued. Gradually a concept emerged called preventive maintenance. It was discovered that shutting down machines for short periods for scheduled minor maintenance, such as lubrication and adjustments, prevented unscheduled major break-downs for long periods. In the airline business preventive maintenance is the only way to maintain aircraft.

As common as this practice is today, some managers continue to resist preventive maintenance in their operations because they can't afford to lose productivity caused by short shutdown periods. They can't afford to lose a little bit of productivity now; they can only afford to lose a lot of productivity later on.

Preventive maintenance is an intervention to maintain equipment efficiency. It is the mechanic's intervention of physically manipulating mechanical elements, such as aligning tools and adjusting speeds and feed mechanisms, which results in the machine's appropriate output. It keeps things running right. We discovered that this practical approach to managing things is just as effective and necessary in managing people's performance in the form of preventive management.

PREVENTIVE MANAGEMENT IS THE INTERVENTION OF MANIPULATING ELEMENTS IN A SPECIFIC WORK ENVIRONMENT TO BRING ABOUT A PREDICTED OUTCOME THAT WOULD NOT HAVE HAPPENED WITHOUT THAT INTERVENTION.

It keeps things running right by denying people the opportunity to fail.

MANAGEMENT IS AN INTERVENTION

For managers to be effective, management philosophies and theories have to be converted into things managers "do" that influence people's performance.

Management has to be recognized as an intervention the same way mechanical maintenance, cake baking, or orchestra conducting is an intervention to assure a desired outcome. Without the intervention of the baker in cake baking, the ingredients would remain in their cartons and containers. The baker's intervention of mixing, adding specific amounts of certain ingredients in a certain order, plus the baking process results in the desired cake. In musical orchestration, although the music is written, it is the conductor's intervention during practices, together with his direction and control during the performance, which creates the concert.

Applying management as an intervention means that managers must do specific things at specific times to influence the eventual outcome of their people's performance. As in baking a cake, if the manager doesn't do the right things at the right time or in the right sequence, or does them too frequently or not frequently enough, performance outcomes will not be as expected. This is painfully clear when matching the reasons for nonperformance with their preventive solutions in the previous chapters. Hiring the right people is certainly important when staffing any job. However, the most important activity is the manager's interventions, after the person has been hired, manipulating as necessary all those elements in the environment that will produce the expected performance. As with cake baking and concerts, buying the best cooking ingredients or hiring the best musicians alone does not guarantee a good cake or concert.

The good news is that there are only sixteen reasons for poor performance no matter what the job is or what level it is at, and you will never have all sixteen reasons affecting any person at the same time. And if you eliminate all of those reasons for nonperformance, you are left with perfect performance.

Our search for a systematic approach for eliminating these reasons for nonperformance revealed that some of these reasons occur only before the work begins and some of them occur only after the work begins. Obviously, if you don't eliminate those reasons for nonperformance that occur before the work begins, you will be faced with them after the work has begun. The chart in Table 1 separates the reasons into *Before* and *After* categories.

Notice that three items appear on both lists: "Personal Problems," "They Think Something Else Is More Important," and "Obstacles Beyond Their Control." Personal problems can occur at any time. Obstacles can arise and priorities can change after the work begins. The pressure of changing demands from several sources can influence employees to incorrectly interpret what the most important task might be on any day even though they knew what was most important before the work began.

Your *preventive management* strategy is to counteract these reasons for nonperformance before and after the work begins to prevent them from becoming causes of nonperformance. Therefore, your management interventions as solutions fall into two categories, as shown in Table 2. In the *Before* category are those things you do before people begin work. To deal with this category requires you to discuss work in more detail with your employees before they begin an important task or project. This is called work planning.

Table 1
Why Employees Don't Do What
They Are Supposed To Do

Before the Work Begins

B-1 — They don't know what they are supposed to do.
B-2 — They don't know how to do it.
B-3 — They don't know why they should do it.
B-4 — They think your way will not work.
B-5 — They think their way is better.
B-6 — They think something else is more important.
B-7 — They anticipate future negative consequences.
B-8 — Personal problems.
B-9 — Personal limits.
B-10— Obstacles beyond their control.
B-11 — No one could do it.

Table 1
After the Work Begins

A-1—They think they are doing it.
A-2—No positive consequence to them for doing it.
A-3—There are obstacles beyond their control.
A-4—They think something else is more important.
A-5—They are punished for doing what they are supposed to do.
A-6—They are rewarded for not doing it.
A-7—No negative consequence to them for performing badly.
A-8—Personal problems.

It is your *preventive management* delivery system before the work begins, and it goes way beyond, "Have this completed by the 30th and let me know if you have any problems." The importance of the outcome of the task or project dictates the importance of your discussion before the work begins. With a repetitive project a work-planning discussion may take only a minute to cover B-1: when to begin it, when to end it, and what finished should look like. With a larger infrequent project or one this person has never done before your discussion might embrace B-1 through B-11 from Table 2. If you listen during these work-planning discussions, you will get a lot of prompting from your employee, such as, "Why does this have to be done?"

Table 2.
Preventive Management
What to Do Before the Work Begins

B-1 — Let them know what they are supposed to do.

B-2 — Find out if they know how to do it.

B-3 — Let them know why they should do it.

B-4 — Convince them that your way will work.

B-5 — If their way is not better, explain convincingly why it is not better.

B-6 — Let them know the work priorities.

B-7 — Convince them that anticipated future negative consequences for attempting to perform will not occur.

B-8 — Work around personal problems or give the work to someone else.

B-9 — Verify that the work is not beyond their personal limits.

B-10— Verify that there are no obstacles beyond their control.

B-11 — Verify that it can be done.

Table 2.

What to Do After the Work Begins

A-1—Give them performance feedback specifically
and frequently.

A-2—Verbally reward good performance specifically
and frequently.

A-3—Remove obstacles or give employees a strategy
for going around obstacles.

A-4—Let them know the work priorities.

A-5—Remove negative consequences for good
performance or balance them with positive
reinforcement.

A-6—Remove positive consequences for poor
performance.

A-7—Use negative consequences only with consistent poor performance (progressive discipline).

A-8—Work around personal problems or give the
work to someone else.

"It's not my job," "I don't think it will work," "I've got
other more important things to do." But now when you
hear these comments you will deal with them as real
questions and not merely gripes.

In the *After* category are things you do after they
begin work to maintain appropriate performance;
this is called follow-up.

"FOLLOW-UP IS FINDING OUT IF PEOPLE ARE DOING WHAT
THEY ARE SUPPOSED TO BE DOING WHEN THEY ARE SUPPOSED
TO BE DOING IT."

Some people refer to this as "checking up" or "moni-
toring" performance and don't do it because they

don't have the time or don't want people to feel they are not trusted.

Follow-up is your *preventive management* delivery system after the work begins. See the list on Table 2, A-1 through A-8. If you don't follow up on people's performance, you are avoiding the most important part of your management job. The two purposes of follow-up are:

1. To maintain performance (if performance is appropriate)

   A-2 Reward good performance

2. To improve performance (if performance is inappropriate)

   A-1 Give them performance feedback
   A-3 Remove obstacles
   A-4 Let them know priorities
   A-5 Remove negative consequences for good performance
   A-6 Remove positive consequences for poor performance
   A-7 Use negative consequences for poor performance
   A-8 Work around personal problems

Notice that the interventions A-1, A-2, and A-5 in Table 2 would not occur if you, as the manager, intervened only when problems occurred. This should have a dramatic effect on your interpretation of follow-up and how often it should be done. Currently, managers tend to follow up or check up only when alerted by a problem. But follow-up is needed periodically as *performance maintenance* even when things seem to be progressing well. When you wait for problems to occur before you intervene, you are using reactive management, always a little too late. If you follow up on your employees' activities, providing assistance and consequences to maintain appropriate performance, you will be intervening with *preventive management,* that is, preventing people from failing. You will be using proactive management and will be faced with fewer performance problems.

Because *preventive management* takes time, you should do it only when and where performance is important to you or your organization. A good method of judging importance is to place a value on the cost of failure. If the cost of employee failure is negligible, spend very little time managing it. For example, if employees' late arrival for work has no harmful effect on their performance or service to others, don't waste your time managing it. Or if your company sells a one-of-a-kind product or service and customers buy it no matter how you treat them and you are not worried about competition, don't spend a lot of time managing customer service. On the other hand, if employees' late arrival hurts production or poor customer service so alienates your exclusive customers that all of them will desert you when a competitive product enters the marketplace, spend a lot of time managing those things. As mentioned in the introduction, management is an intervention more like bridge building than rain dancing: there is a direct cause-effect relationship between a manager's interventions and an employee's performance.

The happy state of affairs is that if you eliminate all the reasons why people don't do what they are supposed to do, you are left with appropriate performance.

18

The Importance
of Friendliness

THERE IS ONE MORE IMPORTANT ELEMENT YOU CAN CONTROL that influences your success as a manager. It is not something managers told us about; it is something we observed managers doing. Effective managers use it frequently, and ineffective managers rarely use it. We call it friendliness.

You have probably heard it said that managers' success is directly related to their relationships with the people working for them, the people working with them, and the people they work for. This is true. In analyzing these relationships we found that each relationship can be separated into two general categories: there are the business relationship and the person-to-person relationship. The second category deals with that important element we called friendliness, the little things effective managers do on a person-to-person basis that bad managers rarely do.

Friendliness doesn't mean being your employees' best friend, or forgiving bad performance, understanding personal problems, inviting them to your home, lending them money, or letting them do what they want to do. Friendliness means doing the little things you might think of as politeness and respect, such as:

○ Saying please and thank you

○ Looking at people's faces when they are talking to you and showing a pleasant face

○ Greeting people with a good morning or a good afternoon before talking about their work

○ Being prompt in keeping appointments so people don't have to waste time waiting for you

○ Treating people who come into your office as guests by not making them wait or talk to the top of your head while you finish your paperwork and by asking them if they will forgive you if you have to take a minute or two to complete your paperwork

○ Apologizing when you are late or have to interrupt a meeting

○ Not insulting them and wasting their time by accepting nonrelated phone calls during meetings

○ Holding conversations with people versus lecturing them and not interrupting people when they are speaking

- Controlling your emotional outburst because you don't have the right to speak loudly or otherwise abuse your employees
- Not making sarcastic comments
- Not eating or drinking while meeting with your employees unless you offer them the same privilege

These things are easy enough to do once you decide to do them.

There is another aspect of this friendliness that can only be described generally as showing interest or getting to know people. We saw managers talking to their employees about the employees' personal interests and outside work activities, such as hobbies, sports, family events such as anniversaries, birthdays, graduations, purchases of new cars, appliances, or houses, and any other social activities that are appropriate to discuss. But these discussions rarely lasted more than a few minutes and sometimes were as brief as, "How did you do in bowling last night?" or "I hope your daughter does well in tonight's gymnastic competition." It was not the length of the discussion that seemed important, it was the fact that the manager knew of the event and took the time to mention it.

This friendliness category is not evident to the casual observer because effective managers do not switch from "Let's talk about the business stuff" to "Let's talk about the friendly stuff." Their friendliness is threaded throughout their business activities by the hour, by the day. The managers we identified as having this "friendliness" just seemed to be nice people.

They smile a lot, they are easy to talk to, they are polite, thoughtful of others, and considerate as they perform their management interventions. It just seems so natural when they do it.

Unfortunately, there are some managers who aren't friendly at work because they are not pleasant people in the first place; they are not even friendly to their families or neighbors. Some people are only friendly to their dog. But there are a lot of other managers who are naturally nice to their families and friends and neighbors, but when they arrive at work, they change; they become unnatural and unfriendly. When I mention this to managers who do that, they say, "You are right; I don't know what comes over me at work. I guess I get so busy, there doesn't seem to be time for friendliness." It should be just the opposite; if something comes over you at work, it should be friendliness.

If you want to be more successful than you are, spend some time acting friendly at work; it doesn't take more time to smile. When discussing this in a seminar one manager said, "But I'm not exactly the friendliest person in the world. How can I become more friendly on the job?" I told him that the first thing in the morning and several times each workday he should say to himself, "All of the people working for me are millionaires and don't have to work for me one minute longer than they want to, so I better act nice to them." He later told me that he began saying that to himself as he got out of his car in the company parking lot and it reminded him to say "thank you" and "please" more often.

As important as friendliness is, I want to make sure you are not misled into believing that friendliness will replace or correct poor management. I have seen effective managers who didn't use this friendliness element but could have been more effective if they did use it. I have seen very friendly managers who were ineffective because they were not doing effective management things. In other words, managers who intervene effectively in a friendly way are always more effective than managers who intervene effectively in a nonfriendly way. Maintaining a friendly relationship is another part of maintaining work performance. It also helps you avoid having people try to hurt you because they don't like you. It might save your life.

19

Questions
and Answers

Q: It appears that all of these reasons for nonperformance are caused by what the manager does or fails to do. Isn't this placing too much responsibility on the manager for any individual's performance?

A: If you talk about the placement of responsibility, you could draw up a nice organizational chart and allocate percentages of responsibility to each individual on the chart. But when you talk about solving a problem, the question is *who* should be taking *what* action to *solve* that problem. If you can picture an organization with one employee and one boss and the employee is performing badly, the question is, "Who must take the first action to correct that problem?" The employee certainly must do the work, but who must act to change all those elements in the work environment that affect the worker's performance?

The one who loses the most when an employee fails is the manager; the one who gains the most when an employee performs well is the manager. Since management is an intervention, it is the manager who must intervene to assist the employee in performing appropriately. Stop talking about responsibility and start talking about who is supposed to make the first move to improve the situation. The answer is the boss.

Q: But aren't you asking the boss to do everything?

A: No, not everything. The boss hires, trains, and manages the employee to achieve appropriate performance. When the employee performs inappropriately, the manager applies corrective efforts to improve performance, and if the performance doesn't improve, the manager fires the employee. The employee gets paid to work; the manager gets paid to manage the employee to work.

Q: But suppose you eliminate all these reasons for nonperformance and the employee is still not performing appropriately. What do you do then?

A: The next thing to do is to hold a coaching discussion, which is described in my book *Coaching for Improved Work Performance*.[5] And if that doesn't work, then demote, transfer, or terminate the person or learn to live with the problem.

Q: You say that these are all the reasons why people at work don't do what they are supposed to do, but you don't talk about attitudes.

A: When managers talk about employees' poor attitude, they are either labeling behavior they don't like or referring to employees' thoughts which are allegedly reflected in the undesirable behavior. Neither of these provide any useful basis for improving any one's performance for the following reasons.

1. When you refer to good or bad attitude you are merely labeling something in general terms, saying nothing specific about the behavior or the thought.

2. When you label people's thoughts because of their actions, you don't know what you are talking about. You are merely guessing what their thoughts might be. You didn't see the thoughts; you only saw the behavior.

3. There is some relationship between thoughts and action, but it is erroneous to believe that actions are reflections of thoughts. Some people don't like what they are doing, so they do it perfectly or fast so they will not have to do it again or can quickly go on to something else they like better. Some people like what they are doing so much, they never finish it. Some people make a fuss or pout only because it gets them attention from the boss. Some people cause trouble for the boss only because it gets them hero status from fellow workers. And how about one of life's truths, "You only hurt the ones you love"?

4. When you say someone has a poor attitude, you are labeling him and shifting both the blame and the source of corrective action from you to him. If he has a poor attitude, then he is the one who must change. You have no reason to take preventive action, since it is not your fault.

The concept of attitude as related to performance appeared in the field of psychology around 1840. But to date there is no agreement among psychologists as to what attitude is, how to measure it, and what, if any, influence it has on performance.

When someone starts talking about another person's attitude, ask, "How do you know that; what do they say or do which leads you to conclude they have that attitude?" Their answer will eventually describe behavior which you can analyze and change using *preventive management.*

You can deal with people's thoughts to some degree when you communicate *reasons* why people should do things and let them *understand* the *consequences* of doing it right and doing it wrong. You also deal with people's thoughts when you explain to them that the pain they anticipate for doing a certain thing will really not occur. But you would be talking about specific thoughts. Talking about attitude doesn't help you or your employees, so avoid it.

Q: You also haven't discussed motivation. Where does that fit in?

A: Motivation is an old idea in psychology which was created to describe what we don't know causes people to do what they do. It is a generalized idea that something is going on inside the person although we don't know what it is and can't measure it. It's not like blood pressure. Research psychologists are very careful when discussing motivation if they discuss it at all, but the rest of the world treats it like the air we breathe. How many times each day do you hear, "She is not motivated," "He has lost his motivation," "I feel motivated," "This will motivate them," "This will demotivate them," "He is a motivator," "We are looking for a motivated person," "You have to motivate them"?

The sad truth is that the people saying these things are talking about something but don't know what it is. If you asked them, "How do I motivate someone?" you would wander further into the land of non-specifics and metaphors, such as "Have them buy in," "Get them dedicated." If you keep asking, "How do I do that?" and they don't get frustrated with how dumb they think you are, they will eventually stumble onto many of the sixteen influences on performance you just learned.

If you deal with the practical aspects of what influences people's performance, you don't need the word "motivation" and will be dealing with most of those things other consultants tell you will improve motivation (however they measure that). Experience has demonstrated that if you eliminate all the reasons why people don't do what they are supposed to do, the only thing you have left is appropriate performance.

Q: What is wrong with "ownership," or wanting people to "buy in" and "be dedicated"?

A: These ideas have a nice ring to them, but these terms are nonspecific and don't appear in formal psychological research findings. You can't trick people into believing they own something which they do not own. And people only become dedicated for reasons such as love/hate, blood (family), religion, survival, and occasionally their country. You can find people with fixations and obsessions and compulsions who put work ahead of health and family, but this is not normal; work, after all, is only work.

A popular video about productivity and motivation praised a large international business machine company for having the ability to create in its employees "a consuming interest in doing their job." This sounds laudable when you first hear it, but what is "a consuming interest"? Consuming means that at the end of a process there is less than what you began with. Does this mean that the employees in that company have so much interest in doing their job that their personal life, their health, family, whatever, is consumed by the job? Why would any one think this is a good idea? You can expect and require employees to do 100 percent of what you pay for but not to be consumed in the process.

Studies of human behavior have revealed that if you involve employees in a discussion about the work or project before they begin work, they will work harder or longer at doing those tasks. The employees and manager tend to describe the result of these discussions as having "buy-in" or "ownership," which is why they work harder. However, when you examine in detail what was discussed in the prework meeting and compare that with the list (Table 2) of what managers should do before the work begins, you will discover a lot of similarity.

If, before the work begins, you let people know what they are supposed to do by discussing the problem, as well as the solution, and let them know why they should do it, and discuss their ideas and why their ideas may not work, and discuss your own ideas and why they will work, and you let them know the importance of this task relative to other tasks, and you discover obstacles that could prevent them from performing and you discuss what they don't know how to do, and you give them guidelines for knowing (feedback) if they are doing it, you will be using *preventive management* interventions. If you did these things and you got improved performance, you might conclude that you caused your employees to have "buy-in" or "ownership," but you couldn't measure that.

The key to success as a manager is intervening effectively, doing the right things at the right time. If you now conduct participative management meetings, you are unknowingly dealing with some of the reasons why employees don't do what they are supposed to do. If you follow the list in Table 2 during those meetings, you will not leave anything out and you will be even more successful. But if you don't follow up and deal with the reasons which occur after the work begins, you will not be as successful as you could be.

If you give your employees a stake in your company and share the profits with them, you will get their attention as owners but you will still have to manage them to get what you pay for.

Q: It seems to me there are a lot more things going on in the work environment than you mentioned here. For example, there are organizational changes, political infighting, retirement situations, major fluctuations in the economy, inflation, and technological innovations. Aren't you oversimplifying things?

A: No, I am not oversimplifying things. The subject of this book is *preventive management*. It is directed toward the interventions within your control that will eliminate all of the reasons why people at work don't do what they are supposed to do. This is not a book on formal training, job instructions, labor negotiation, wage and salary administration, strategic planning, financial management, corporate acquisition, or psychological counseling. It merely deals directly with a specific set of circumstances that commonly exist throughout any work environment at all levels and that are predominantly not managed with intention by most managers. If you view those things you mentioned, such as political infighting and technological innovations, as consequences and obstacles to performance, you could deal with them more effectively.

Q: I also notice you don't talk about job satisfaction. Where does job satisfaction fit in as an influence on performance?

A: Workers, journalists, and amateur psychologists talk a lot about job satisfaction. I don't talk about job satisfaction because I am not aware of validated research studies that show a direct relationship between job satisfaction and work performance. One of the problems with job satisfaction is that there is no universal definition of what it is or how to measure it.

However, if you avoid attempts to measure generalizations such as employee dedication, commitment, and loyalty and concentrate on the specific aspects of the work relationship, you can learn a lot and improve performance. Recent studies have shown a correlation between employee job satisfaction survey results and customer satisfaction. The message was that increases in job satisfaction result in increased customer satisfaction. But the companies measuring job satisfaction and making changes to improve it are not actually dealing with employee general happiness. They are dealing with employees' opinions about work processes such as fair workload distribution, schedule flexibility, and internal communications. Frequently the so-called job satisfaction or attitude surveys in retail organizations reveal that employees want more information about customer levels of satisfaction and a more detailed understanding of customer needs. The former shows that employers do not have frequent enough or specific enough *feedback* about their work. The latter shows that employees do not know *what* they are supposed to do or *how* to satisfy customer needs.

These are work process problems, not worker satisfaction problems. Worker dissatisfaction is the symptom, not the problem. Making workers happier would not solve the performance problems; solving the performance problems would accidentally make some workers happier. The surveys linking improved job satisfaction with improved customer satisfaction are actually linking improved work processes and employee knowledge with customer satisfaction.

Surveys are good for collecting data, but bad surveys give you bad data. If you call it a job satisfaction survey, you will ask some bad questions and try to come up with some kind of overall happiness score. If you call it a work analysis survey or performance improvement survey, you will ask the right questions and have no need for an overall score. As an example, our Manager Coaching Survey which we conduct for companies twice a year looks like this.

	Usually	Sometimes	Seldom
My manager gives me clear instructions.	_____	_____	_____
My manager is available when I need assistance.	_____	_____	_____

	Usually	Sometimes	Seldom
My manager explains the reason for projects and changes.	_____	_____	_____
My manager's responses are unpredictable.	_____	_____	_____
My manager gives helpful suggestions.	_____	_____	_____
My manager praises good work.	_____	_____	_____
When talking about performance problems, he/she concentrates on performance, not me personally.	_____	_____	_____
My manager lets me speak without interruption.	_____	_____	_____

You can see that answers to specific questions like these provide valuable feedback to each manager. It's like seeing your bowling score but is even better because it points out exactly what behavior must be improved. If your objective is to improve performance, you only need to identify what behavior must change; an overall score is useless.

The other aspect of job satisfaction is individual employees telling you that they don't like their job or that it is no fun. If someone really does not like her job, she should change it. Life is too short to spend all day doing something you don't like. But not liking a job is different from "It's no fun." Most people like their job in the beginning because it is new and at least they are happy to have one. It is also easy to like a job when you are learning something new. Some jobs are easy to like forever because they are like the company softball game: there is a lot of winning and losing throughout the day, making it exciting. However, it is sad but true that most jobs are repetitive, boring, and no fun at all after the first three months. Even the things we like to do in life would become boring and no fun if we had to do them every day, all day like a job.

The reason we have to pay people for work is because it is work and people would rather be doing something else. If all the work in your organization was fun, you could call it an amusement park and charge people to come to work. If you can help someone change a job he doesn't like, do it. But don't be wary of telling people who don't like their jobs, "It is okay not to like it, but it is not okay to fail to do it."

Job satisfaction, however you describe it, can go up and down by the hour independently of the work performance. In other words, it is possible for low-performing workers to have a high job satisfaction and high-performing workers to have low job satisfaction. It would be more relevant for you to think of the rewards or punishments people receive (or don't receive) daily for doing specific things at work.

Q: In the section where you talk about managers using verbal compliments to deliver a positive consequence following people's appropriate performance, are you suggesting that people will work for nothing if you only give them verbal compliments?

A: There are a lot of situations in life where people actually work hard when there is no possibility of receiving money for it, such as volunteer work for communities and churches and social organizations. People even work hard in leisure sports even though these activities are painful and punishing to perform and are not paid for. I am not suggesting, however, that verbal rewards will get people to work in your company without pay. We all pay people to work for us. The question is, "What influential rewards can you use as a manager to get them to do what you pay them to do?" The answer is, "Your specific verbal reinforcement in the form of compliments for good or improved performance."

Q: If I had a worker who was coming to work late every day because he was going through a divorce, I don't think I would feel comfortable telling him that I require him to come to work on time in spite of his personal problems.

A: It is interesting that you would not do what you are supposed to do because you would consider that punishing (uncomfortable) to you. The interesting question is, Would you tell that person to come to work on time if your boss said you would be fired if you didn't solve the problem?

There are other relevant factors to consider here. First of all, how many days in a row has the person been late for work? Also, is he late two minutes a day or forty-two minutes a day? Third, if he is late in the morning, how much damage does that do to job performance? Is it also possible and appropriate to make up lost time at the end of the day, or does the job suffer drastically because of the lost time? How long does it appear the lateness problem is going to continue? The answers to these questions would tell you how long you can let the situation continue or whether you must take action now to correct it. In the final analysis, if the problem is severe and it must be corrected, it is okay for you to feel uncomfortable, but it is not okay for you to fail to correct the problem.

Q: The idea of listing all of the behaviors a person is supposed to perform on a job sounds appropriate, but does the job description have to include everything the person does?

A: If you pay somebody to behave in a certain way, that behavior must be recorded somewhere, either on the job description or in a procedure manual you can refer to in the job description. For example, in the job description it is okay to say, "When operating the electron microscope, follow the prescribed procedures in the manual SOP27," or, "When filing expense reports, follow the procedures specified in Accounting Procedures SOP56."

Q: Hasn't teamwork been successful without management intervention?

A: The natural process of creating a team accidentally deals with these sixteen influences on performance. The first thing team members ask is, "What do you want us to do?" The discussion then leads to why it should be done, the obstacles preventing performance, confessions of not knowing how to do something, clearing up whose way will work, and identifying priorities. Teams also create specific and high-frequency feedback, work around personal problems, and reward and punish each other for good and bad performance. The team members are dealing with the sixteen reasons instead of the manager. There is no magic in teamwork; the people who tout it are merely not aware of the actual interventions influencing performance. For that matter, there is no mystery or magic in managing people; if you don't know what is causing good or bad performance, you are merely not examining all of the influences on performance. As mentioned earlier, management is an intervention whether you are managing people or managing things. If you are not intervening, performance is occurring without your help. What is described here is a proactive system of *preventive management* rather than a reactive process of problem management. With preventive management, your interventions will maintain performance, preventing problems from occurring.

You might conclude at this point that if you do the necessary things to prevent these reasons for non-performance from occurring, there will be very few people in your organization failing. That observation is correct and certainly consistent with one definition of management, which is,

> "Management is doing those things necessary to deny people who work for you the unpleasant opportunity of failing."

This definition is especially important when the cost of failure is important to both the organization and the employee. So don't waste time trying to get inside people's heads. All of the good and bad performances (except equipment failure) which happen in your organization are done by some individual person. If what the employees do is not managed, performance will be accidental: sometimes good, sometimes bad. You have the ability to control the influences on performance to orchestrate more good performance and eliminate the accidents. Do what you are supposed to do: Be an effective manager by eliminating all those reasons why people fail; you will be noted for the successes of the people you manage.

Q: Where does *empowerment* fit into *preventive management?*

A: Empowerment is merely the process of permitting (encouraging) lower-level employees to make decisions which were formerly made by people higher up in the organization. The employees assigned/ granted this new decision-making authority are closer to the work process they are deciding about and are usually knowledgeable enough to be able to make appropriate decisions. This speeds up the decision-making process and sometimes the decisions are better than they might have been. A secondary effect is that employees gain more satisfaction/reward in completing a task without approval from above and may feel more important and valuable because they are in control of a process; they seem more interested in their work. Gone is the frustration of not being able to finish something because a decision has not yet come down from above.

However, the idea of *empowerment* has taken on a more general meaning similar to motivation, alluding to some quasimagical effect it has on employees. Pushing decisions downward is an organizational change as well as a job change and is a good thing to do. But it is only one management intervention which will put more winning and losing in the employee's work world.

Q: Should I trust my employees?

A: That depends on what you mean by trust. If it means that you believe your employees are basically honest and are willing to give you a full day's work for a full day's pay, that is fine. But if it means that you don't have to follow up (check on) your employees' performance because you trust them, it's a bad idea. Your trust would be a reason for you to not manage them. Remember that follow-up has the two purposes of (1) maintaining performance if it is appropriate, and (2) helping to improve performance if it is inappropriate. If you don't follow up because you trust them, you would not discover or deal with all the reasons for inappropriate performance which occur after the work begins that have nothing to do with dishonesty.

Sometimes when you follow up, people will say, "Don't you trust me?" You can say, "What I am doing is called follow-up; it's what I get paid to do."

I wish good management to you.

Endnotes

1. Ferdinand F. Fournies, *Coaching for Improved Work Performance* (Blue Ridge Summit, PA: TAB Books, 1987).

2. Ferdinand F. Fournies, *Performance Appraisal-Design Manual* (Bridgewater, NJ: F. Fournies & Associates, Inc., 1983).

3. Ferdinand F. Fournies, *Coaching for Improved Work Performance.*

4. Ferdinand F. Fournies, *Why Customers Don't Do What You Want Them to Do—And What to Do About It* (New York: McGraw-Hill, 1994).

5. Ferdinand F. Fournies, *Coaching for Improved Work Performance.*

Index

163

165

About the Author

Ferdinand F. Fournies is an international management consultant specializing in programs to improve human productivity in business. He enjoys the controversy of exposing useless people-management concepts and presenting practical alternatives. In addition to his books about coaching employees and improving sales-call effectiveness, his research has exposed performance appraisal programs as a waste of time and has developed functional solutions. He has been a guest lecturer for Columbia University Graduate School of Business for 14 years and instructor for the MBA Program at Fairleigh Dickinson University.